GIRL BOSS

1359

Running the Show Like the Big Chicks

Entrepreneurial Skills, Stories, and Encouragement for Modern Girls

By Stacy Kravetz

Foreword by Gillian Anderson

Designed by Amy Inouye

ISBN: 0-9659754-2-8
Library of Congress Catalog-in-Publication Number: 99-60818

GIRL PRESS

slightly dangerous books for girl mavericks

GIRL PRESS books are available for retail distribution through:
LPC Group
1436 West Randolph Street
Chicago, IL 60607
(312) 432-7650

GIRL PRESS books are available at special quantity discounts to use as premiums, sales promotions, or for use in education programs. For more information, please write the Director of Special Sales, GIRL PRESS, PO Box 480389, Los Angeles, CA 90048.

Ms. Foundation for Women
TAKE OUR DAUGHTERS TO WORK

A portion of the proceeds from GIRL BOSS will be donated to the Ms. Foundation for Women, sponsor of Take Our Daughters to Work® Day.

*"You will do foolish things,
but do them with enthusiasm."*

—French writer COLLETTE

Cleopatra

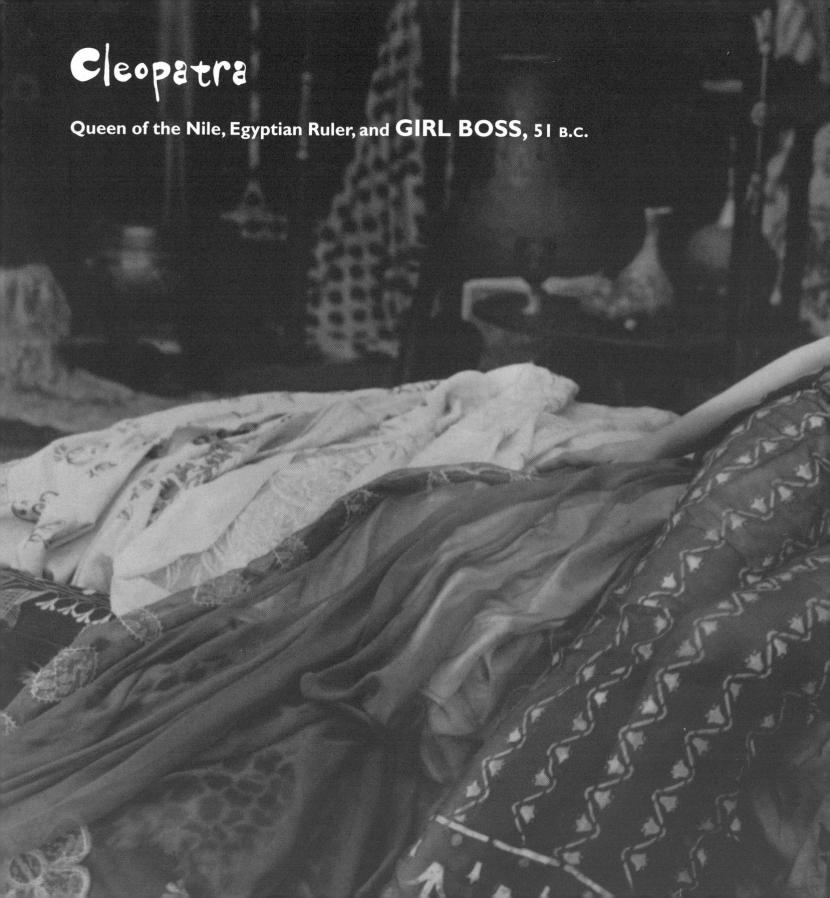

Queen of the Nile, Egyptian Ruler, and GIRL BOSS, 51 B.C.

Theda Bara in the film *Cleopatra* (Fox, 1917)

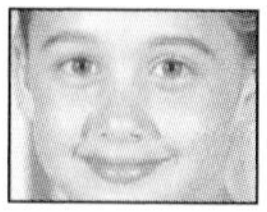

SECTION 1

What You Need to Know

You Can Do It!

SECTION 2

Getting Started

SECTION 3

Ideas for Your Biz

SECTION 4

Getting the Word Out

SECTION 5

Dollar Smart

SECTION 6

Advice from Girl Bosses

Foreword

I'm not sure exactly where I got my drive and perseverance—perhaps my father, an entrepreneur and perfectionist—but it began at an early age. At school, I would always take on the most challenging projects, sometimes to the degree that I would lose interest before they were completed. I have since learned to keep my goals realistic, and to only take on tasks which I know I can complete.

One project I did follow through on and which, consequently, was empowering and inspiring for me was directing a play in high school. I have no idea what compelled me to take on the challenge but I did it and I did it all. I directed it, produced it, built the sets, and designed the programs on my father's computer.

It was so much fun, and the experience awakened me to the knowledge that I could do anything I set my mind to. I believe this of everyone. I believe from the bottom of my heart that there is nothing we as human beings, and especially we as women cannot tackle. It is not a matter of being fearless. The fear is sometimes constant but it's about moving forward regardless of the fear. Courage means feeling the fear and doing it anyway.

One of my only role models as a young woman was Meryl Streep and, specifically, her character in *Out of Africa.* I would watch the movie whenever I needed inspiration because Ms. Streep so brilliantly portrayed an incredibly courageous woman who stands alone to save her plantation. Her performance and the strength of her character were tangible examples of how I wanted to be in the world, and I soaked it in and learned from her experience.

Which brings me to *The X-Files.* When I was cast as Special Agent Dana Scully, I had no idea what I was doing or what I was getting myself into—I was terrified. But I knew that there was one thing I could rely on, and that was that I felt I knew how to act, and that I would be robbing myself of an incredible experience if I didn't just jump in head first. So I did. And let me tell you, every single minute of every day we shot the pilot episode, I was convinced they were going for fire me. I even started to question my talent which made it even scarier. Fortunately, with the love and support of a close friend who kept convincing me to just show up and do the best that I could do, I hung in there. And I survived! I didn't know anything about acting in front of a camera but I learned. I learned to trust my instincts and commit fully to my choices, that there are no wrong decisions and that even "bad" decisions aren't fatal.

I have been so blessed to portray such a phenomenal woman as Dana Scully. She has taught me about strength and self-worth and personal power. In early episodes, when I was called upon to address large groups of male FBI agents with authority and self assurance, I felt so scared and weak that my voice would come out high-pitched and shaky. But the more I "acted as if" I was self-assured, the more I felt powerful. And believe it or not, it can be that simple.

"Acting as if" is sometimes all it takes to empower oneself, and I have learned to carry this into other areas of my life. When meeting with high-powered directors and producers, or presenting an award at an award ceremony, or doing a talk show; I act as if I am a strong, capable, worthy woman of power. And the more I do this, the more people listen to what I have to say and value my opinion.

Another tool that has been invaluable to me during high-stress situations is prayer. Praying to something greater than myself, whether it's a God or a role model or the ocean, is an immensely empowering device. Just getting quiet for a few moments before the event and asking for guidance and strength in the room; and if you can actually visualize yourself walking into the room as you would like to be, and visualize everything turning out exactly the way you would like it to turn out—you will be amazed at how different you feel. And don't get discouraged. The more practice you have doing this the stronger you will feel, and the more powerful you will find the results.

Another miraculous result of playing Scully has been all the incredible young women I have been blessed to meet along the way—women who have shared that they have received strength from Scully, that because of Scully's strength they have been afraid but done it anyway. These have been women from all walks of life: women from low-income neighborhoods who have persevered despite all odds to study hard and pursue their dreams, enabling them to enter into better schools and work environments; women who have illnesses and physical challenges who have gotten better and stronger because they believe they can. I truly believe that we can overcome any hurdle that lies before us and create the life we want to live. I have seen it happen time and time again.

Now before I get off my soapbox, I want to talk about two other areas I feel important in the life of a powerful woman.

Never lie no matter what the situation. There is no predicament you could ever find yourself in that is worth lying. We need to be responsible for our actions and the only way to live this and learn it is to tell the truth. Other people will then learn that we are trustworthy, and trust is essential in any relationship, business or personal.

Be of service. Whether you make yourself available to a friend or co-worker, or you make time every month to do volunteer work, there is nothing that harvests more of a feeling of empowerment than being of service to someone in need.

Okay, I think I've said everything I wanted to say. Just remember, you can do anything you set your mind to, but it takes action, perseverance, and facing your fears.

Be courageous, believe in yourself, and be the best woman you can be. I'm with you all the way.

Gratefully,

Gillian Anderson

QUIZ: Are You a Girl Boss?

1. **A weekend rolls around** and you've got piles of books you could read and the TV is beckoning from the other room, but all that's on your mind is finding a cool new project to tackle.

2. **You see a cool painted tank top** in a hip store like Urban Outfitters and are tempted to buy it, but then you realize it has a pretty basic design that **you could probably paint yourself.** Instead of pulling out your wallet, you stock up on paint and plain t-shirts and give yourself a weekend of artistic escape.

3. **You're on a tight budget**—allowance doesn't stretch very far and your baby-sitting money isn't going to buy that whole new outfit you want. **So you decide to start a small business** that you can run after school and on weekends.

4. **You can't find** the kind of fun jewelry or hair accessories that you see in a magazine **so you figure out how to make a version** of them yourself.

5. **You like to keep busy** and have energy to burn at the end of the day.

6. **You're ready to tackle the world**—you just need a few tips on how to do it.

DO ANY OF THESE APPLY TO YOU?

Girl Bosses Say YES.

SECTION 1

What You Need to Know

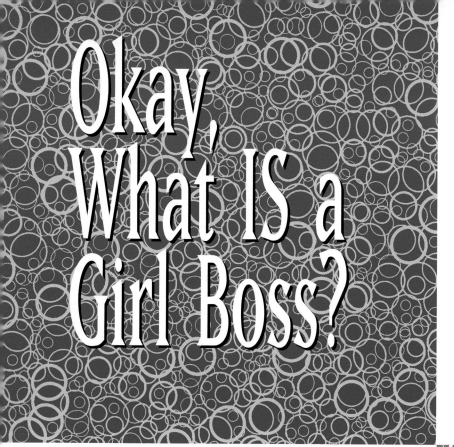

Okay, What IS a Girl Boss?

A Girl Boss doesn't take no for an answer.

A Girl Boss is savvy, she's smart and she's sure of herself. No one needs to tell her what to do because she's already doing it. Sure, she had to figure out how to do it—no one knows everything—but she figured it out by reading the right things, talking to the right people, asking the right questions. Remember—even those Girl Bosses who seem like they were **born** that way had to learn it all somewhere—just like you.

A Girl Boss knows when it's time to take charge.

But a Girl Boss knows how to do it with finesse and flair, and make other people feel smart too. A Girl Boss calls the shots, but knows when to let someone else help her out. She can run with the guys, and she knows when to run faster and farther. A Girl Boss takes pride in her work.

Why be a Girl Boss?

Because if you don't, someone else will. And you'll end up working for her instead of running the show yourself. Look around at all the Girl Bosses with start-up companies—so many small fish in fields like computer design, CD-ROMs, publishing, and the arts—and they're all making it on their own because they had ideas and figured out ways to make them happen.

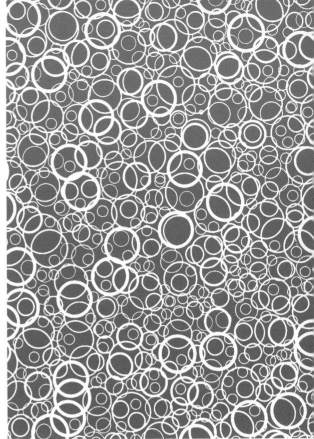

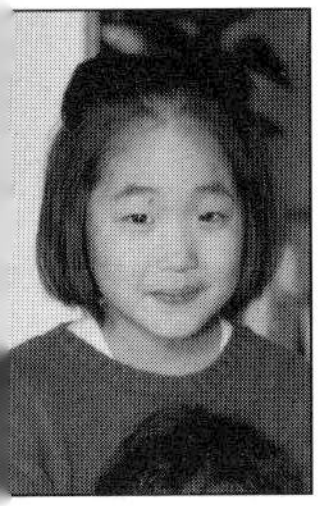

A Girl Boss knows when to get help.

A Girl Boss knows who to go to for advice or a pep talk. A Girl Boss wants to run the show like the big chicks. And a Girl Boss does.

Do you have what it takes to be a Girl Boss?

Of course you do! Why not start now? The sooner you begin, the sooner you'll be on your way to being a super-charged, card-carrying Girl Boss. And everyone will be asking you how **you** did it.

Tricks of the Trade—

What Girl Bosses Know

Being a Girl Boss is a matter of thinking like the big chicks, but knowing how to start small. Learn things the easy way—from the lessons of those who came before you.

Just because you're starting a business or selling your wares, doesn't mean you have to start from scratch. You don't have to touch the stove to know it's hot, so why should you have to get stiffed on a payment to learn that everything needs to be in writing? You can get in on the tricks of the trade for whatever your trade may be. Be creative in finding the answers to the tough questions: use the Internet, scan trade publications and magazines, and call people cold. Most of the time, just asking for information is the best way to get it.

That doesn't mean copying people's ideas outright. It means learning from their techniques—using the things that worked for them to grow your own business. And don't be afraid to ask how they did it. People are proud of their accomplishments and are often happy to tell their success stories. ***Don't be afraid to ask a fellow Girl Boss how she did it.***

I have yet to hear a man ask for advice on how to combine marriage and a career.
—Gloria Steinem

Get Wired!

The Internet is a great resource. Get out your surfboard and type in key words that relate to what you're doing. It's amazing how much information people are willing to give away—for free. The Internet can teach you about the products companies sell or it can help you get hooked up with people through chat rooms. Who knows, you could fall into a whole new business idea just by browsing around, looking at zines and chatting with people doing the same kinds of things that interest you.

Plug in!

Madame C. J. Walker became the first African-American woman millionaire by building an empire based on hair care products. (She's shown here with "Walker agents" who sold her products door-to-door, kind of like Avon ladies today.) A provision in her will stated that her company would always be headed by women.

Girl Boss Tricks:

1

If you don't know how to do it, ask someone who does. There's always someone who has been around longer, made some mistakes and figured things out the hard way. That's the best person to ask for advice so you don't get tripped up with time-consuming-yet-avoidable tasks that **drain away your time and creativity.**

2

If someone asks if you can do something, always say "yes." Say it even if you don't know how to do it—just figure you'll learn how to do it later. Don't worry that you're telling a fat lie—in reality, you can do it, you just need to learn how—so you're being honest when you say "yes" even if it means you have to surf the Internet for three hours and make a dozen phone calls immediately after your meeting to figure it out.

3

If you can't do everything yourself, delegate—that's a business-like way of saying you need to figure out the best uses of your time and find other ways to get the rest done. In other words, don't sweat the small stuff.

4

Be honest with yourself—know your strengths and weaknesses. For example, if you don't have the best memory for little details, keep a list. Carry it with you, mark things off, write more things down, and don't feel like some anal retentive weirdo for doing it. Or if you know you're likely to start dancing in front of the mirror or playing air guitar if you turn on music while you're working, don't turn on the stereo. Then listen all you want once you've finished.

5

If you're not sure, sleep on it. If someone asks you if you want to do something—whether they want you to work for half price until they know you're good or whether they want you to sacrifice all your weekends on a project—take a night to sleep on it. The work will still be there in the morning and you'd be surprised how a good night's sleep changes your perspective.

6

Realize there's always more to learn—Keep informed about what's going on in the world by talking to people—everyone from the people you baby-sit for to your teachers at school—about what they think about new trends. You can do your own field research by asking for people's opinions. Think of it as a free lesson in what's hip and what's not. Just ask what one person thinks and you'll be one step closer to understanding what the majority of people think.

Have Some Attitude

ATTITUDE IS EVERYTHING. Attitude will help you stand up and ask for what you want, and it's what will keep you going when you're about to give up. Attitude is the thing that gets you out of bed on a Saturday morning and inspires you to do something great with your day. In short—Girl Bosses have attitude.

If you walk into a boutique in your neighborhood with a smile on your face and energy in your step, you'll be halfway to getting the store manager to help you. If you want to put a display of t-shirts in their store or show them a catalogue of your work, you'll have a much easier time getting them to say yes if you have a positive, bright attitude.

Convey a message with your smile and your posture. If you walk in with your arms crossed in front of you and a frown on your face, you'll look insecure. You'll have a harder time convincing others to help you if you don't look sure of yourself.

On the other hand, if you smile, speak clearly, and look them in the eye, people will respond. You don't have to go out and take some big self-esteem course to project a good attitude. Just be yourself and assume people will be on your side.

And plan to succeed! Take the attitude that you're giving a store the opportunity to be involved in your business, rather than thinking of it the other way around. Let people know you're building a bright future for your business and they'll want to be a part of it.

QUIZ—Do You Have a Success Mentality?

1 On your first day of trying to sell your fabric coin purses into stores, you encounter a snotty saleswoman who takes one look and says that your purses aren't high enough quality. You:

A Figure she's only one person in one store and don't give up until you find a store that will agree to sell your purses (perhaps on consignment).

B Figure she's got a good point so you go home and try to remake the purses in a high-quality way.

C Worry that all the stores you go to will have that reaction and give up before you've tried.

The answer is **A**! The best thing you could do in this case is keep going from store to store until one agrees to take the purses on consignment for a percentage of the sales price. It will make you feel better once you've gotten one store to agree, and will fuel your drive to go to more.

The problem with answer B is that if you go home and try to reinvent your product each time someone makes a suggestion or doesn't respond positively, you risk spending lots of time and money designing something you hope will please everyone—and never actually selling **anything.**

The problem with answer C is obvious: a defeatist attitude will never get you off the starting blocks. And you've got to start in order to win!

2 You've been spending your free time on weekends putting the beads on the coin purses you want to sell and your friends have noticed that you haven't been around as much. They wonder why. You:

A Try to compensate by spending all your time with them on weekends from now on and forget about your purses.

B Tell them what you've been working on and show them some samples to see if they want to be your first customers.

C Lie and tell them you've been grounded because you're worried that if the coin purses aren't a big hit, everyone will know you tried and failed.

Let's start with the wrong answers. Choosing A would be your first big mistake. After all your hard work it would be crazy and shortsighted to give up on your glamour-gal purses just because you don't want anyone to notice that you're becoming a Girl Boss.

And C is a big fat mistake as well. It's hard, of course, to start something new and have all eyes on your progress. So you don't have to tell everybody in the world. But your friends are your best support and you shouldn't lie to them. Besides, if you don't succeed at the first thing you set out to do, you'll succeed at something else and your **real** friends will be right there cheering all the way.

The best answer is **B**. Be assertive! Inspire your friends to be Girl Boss divas too—maybe they can sell some hot new accessories!

Power Words of Wisdom

- **Think boldly** and in bright colors
- **Innovate:** Make something that doesn't exist
- **Be optimistic** no matter what
- **Consider everything you hear** before blurting out a response
- **Be considerate,** not obnoxious
- **Have fun!**

Setting Goals

Setting goals is important but it's also important to keep them moving. Your goals will change. Something that seemed CRITICAL last year could turn out to be less important once you decide what you really want to do. For example, your goal might be to start an environmental group for a beach clean-up project. But suppose you get involved, and realize that you're even *more* passionate about a rescue fund for sea otters. Your goal could change. The important thing is that you find something you feel passionate about. It doesn't mean you're flaky—just that you're willing to experiment. This is the time to do exactly that!

It's also important to keep track of how you're progressing toward your goals. If you meet some of them, you'll need new goals. And if some look like they'll be impossible to achieve, you might scale back and aim for something more attainable at this stage. Perhaps you'll go back to them later.

Remember too that you don't have to meet your goals immediately. You can have a 5-year or a 10-year plan for yourself and little mini-goals along the way. Just keep something out there to reach for, and don't get discouraged if it takes a while to get it!

The Difference Between Bosses and GIRL BOSSES

Bosses don't want anyone to help them because they're afraid of losing their power.
Girl Bosses know who they can depend on and are grateful when they can share the work.

Bosses think they can't be a friend and a boss.
Girl Bosses know some of their best friends make great workmates.

Bosses are good at saying no.
Girl Bosses don't take no for an answer.

Bosses work with their office doors shut.
Girl Bosses have an open door policy: to let in the best ideas.

Bosses take themselves seriously.
Girl Bosses take other people seriously.

Bosses let you know when they're finished listening to what you have to say.
Girl Bosses listen until you're finished speaking.

Bosses got to where they are by playing by the old rules.
Girl Bosses will get to where they want to go by making up their own rules.

Bosses feel threatened by anyone who does a better job than them.
Girl Bosses seek out those people, knowing they'll only help their business.

What kind of boss do you want to be?

GREAT RESOURCES—Get Plugged In

Idea Cafe is a small business Web site that can help out new and seasoned Girl Bosses by rounding up advice and information. Check it out at **http://www.ideacafe.com**

National Association for Female Executives is the largest organization in the country for businesswomen, whether you run your own business or work for a woman who does. The organization publishes an online version of *Executive Female Magazine* and can be found at **http://www.nafe.com**

American Business Women's Association provides scholarships for women business owners or Girl Bosses like you who want to start them. Plus they publish a cool mag called *Women in Business*. Check them out at **http://www.abwahq.org**

Get ready for the WOWFactor—it's a Web site with all kinds of great ways to help you market your biz. The site promotes lots of great women's businesses and helps you find what you need to make yours grow. **http://www.wowfactor.com**

Women in Technology International is a great site to visit if you're planning on joining the ranks of tech professionals (they're growing like crazy). You can link to other sites by starting at **http://www.witi.com**

At Online Women's Business Resource Center you can learn from the pros. Look for great information about starting or running a business at **http://www.onlinewbc.org**

NetCreations is a great web site to use to promote your business by publishing on the Web. Check it out at **http://www.netcreations.com**

Working Solo is the perfect site for Girl Bosses starting out—when you're running the whole show yourself, it's great to have a place to access resources that show you how to do it. Look for it at **http://www.workingsolo.com**

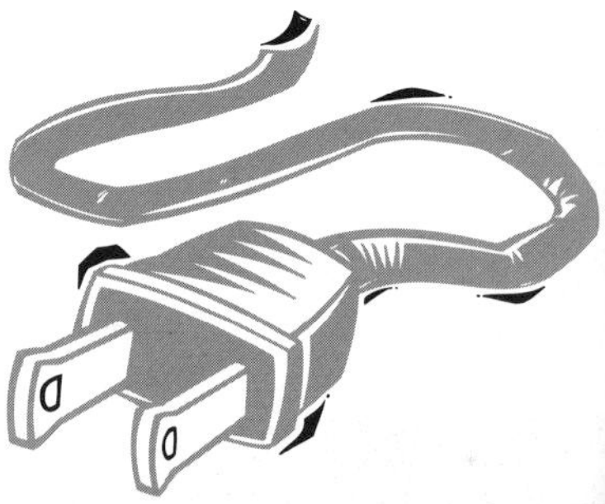

SECTION 2

Getting Started

What Are You Going to Do?

Hmmm...

Sifting Through Ideas and Finding Your Thing

What to do, what to do? If you've got that Girl Boss spirit, but you don't know what to do with all that energy, fear not. This section will help you gather some ideas for great businesses to start, right in your own garage or in a corner of your room.

Start by thinking of what you love to do most— the things you'd do for free if you had all the time in the world. Are you an artist? A writer? An athlete? And what do you like to do for fun? Think about whether you're a whiz on the Internet or a zine reader or a crossword puzzle fanatic or a creative force in the kitchen when no one's around.

Once you've started thinking, put your ideas on paper and keep a list of everything you enjoy. Next try to think about whether any of those things have an application in the biz world; that is, would someone pay you to do them? Try to come up with ways to translate natural talents and enjoyment into small jobs. For example, if you love writing letters to keep up with friends, think about starting a zine of creative observations and funny thoughts. Start putting ideas down for a first issue and draw some illustrations or paste in pictures. Collect a few zines to see how they're done. Make yours just as good, but add something special that the others don't have.

Go the extra mile.

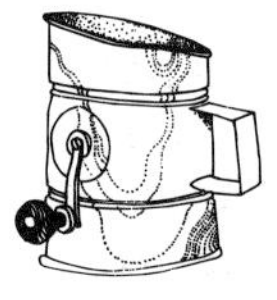

Consider some of the businesses that Girl Bosses just like you call their own: publishing magazines, creating web zines, making short animated films, writing one-act plays, organizing music recitals, making friendship bracelets from colored yarn. Sound like work? Or do these businesses sound more like fun? Find something you love and you can have it all.

After you've made a list of everything you like to do, start to think about how some of those things are real professions. After all, the happiest and most successful people are generally doing what they love,

and many of them loved it before they started doing it for a living.

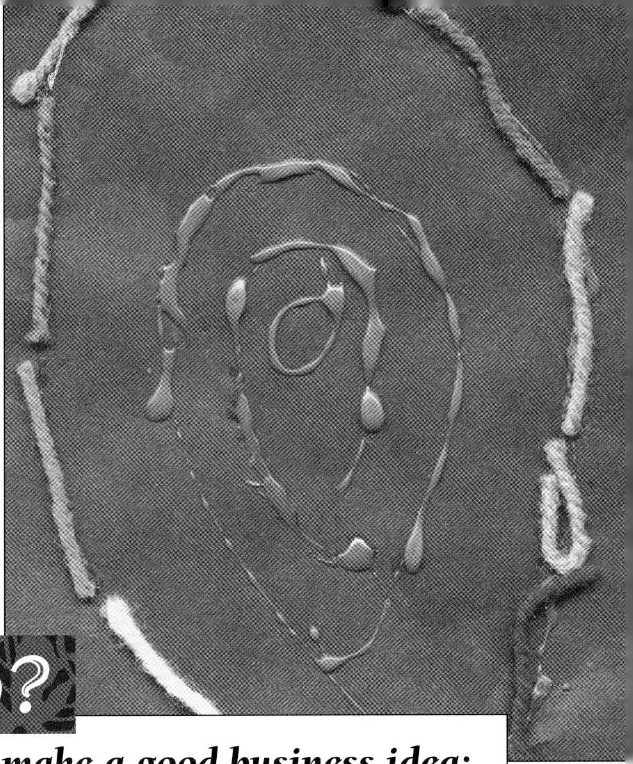

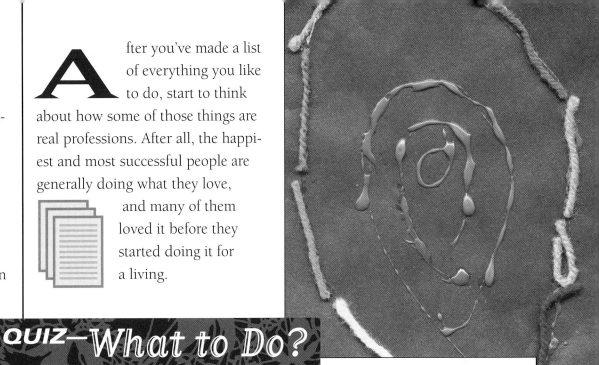

QUIZ—What to Do?

Here's how to decide whether something you enjoy would make a good business idea:

1 ***Your best friend at school has been tutoring her younger brother in math and getting paid $10 an hour by her parents. You know there are other kids his age who need help with math—problem is, math isn't your best subject either. But $10 is $10, right? You:***

A **Put up fliers and pass out notices to mothers when they're picking up kids from school about your new math-tutoring service, figuring you're probably better at it than a bunch of 6th graders.**

B **Realize that math isn't your forte but that creative writing is, and pass out fliers offering to do other kids' writing homework for them.**

C **Put up fliers offering to teach an after-school creative writing class at the elementary schools near you and charge $15 a hour to all the kids who sign up.**

2 **You're painting in art class and accidentally spill paint on one of your new tennis shoes. So you decide to add to the mess and end up splatter-painting the pair. Suddenly, everyone is asking where you got the great pair of painted shoes. You:**

A **Lie and say you got them at a hot new fashion boutique, then pray no one goes there to find you out.**

B **Tell people you did them yourself and say something about how lame you were to have spilled paint in the first place.**

C **Tell people that in a burst of creative inspiration, you painted them and would be happy to do a pair for them—all they have to do is bring you a pair of shoes and $15 and you'll do the rest.**

3 ***You've always wished you had a dog, but your mom won't let you because your younger brother is allergic. You:***

A **Think up creative ways to hook your brother to a leash and walk him around the neighborhood.**

B **Take your walks by yourself and hope you at least run into someone with a dog.**

C **Pass out fliers to your dog-owning neighbors offering your services as a dog walker on weekends or after school. (This works better in urban areas where dogs need to be walked daily.)**

4 **What you really like to do in your free time is head to the mall and hang out with a friend. Unfortunately, this doesn't qualify as a business. But a friend of yours has been trying to get people to come and see her band play this weekend. You:**

A **Go to the mall for the day but promise to come back in time to see her band play.**

B **Skip the mall and sit at home wracking your brains about what kind of Girl Boss biz to start.**

C **Go to the mall and hand out fliers, alternately browsing in stores while you work, in exchange for a small share of what your friend will charge people to come see her band.**

You get the idea—
C will get you farthest in the Girl Boss world!

Do What You Like

How to Turn Your Favorite Hobby into a Biz

Here are some ideas to get your brain thinking like a business goddess:

Do you like sports? See if you can start up an intramural sports league in the sport of your choice. Charge players a small fee to join and post signs at all the schools in your area. Your job will be coordinating game schedules and putting together the teams.

Do you like to cook? See if some place in your neighborhood needs to have baked goods prepared and delivered. Check with barber shops, doctors' offices, and other places where shop owners might want to treat their customers to a sweet snack.

Do you like to watch TV? Consider keeping track of plots and your analyses of various TV shows. Start an Internet web page of your TV reviews. You can keep track of how many hits you get and once your site gets popular, you might be able to get your fans to subscribe . . . for a small fee, of course.

See how easy it can be? It isn't hard to come up with ideas once you start thinking about all the things you like to do. Anything you enjoy could turn out to be a great biz for you.

Do what you love!

What do you need to get started?
Remember—none of the pros woke up one morning as successful Girl Bosses. But they did all have that one day when they got started on their best idea. That's it—just like you. They began with a concept that's probably no better than the one you came up with yourself. Then they transformed that concept into a business.

Here are some tricks to help you gather steam:

1. On a rainy day, instead of making popcorn and watching TV all day, make the popcorn, go into your room and take out your biz notebook. Make lists of the supplies you'll need for your business.
2. On a day when you don't feel like doing anything that has to do with being a Girl Boss, figure out some small step you need to take. Come up with a reward for yourself if you complete it.
3. Take a trip to the bookstore and look through the different sections—cooking, humor, crafts, gardening—whatever—and try to get ideas for the kind of biz you could get excited about.
4. Visit hobby shops, thrift stores, and art supply stores and look for the best supplies at the best prices.
5. Look at catalogues, magazines, and anything else you can get your hands on for ideas about the kinds of things people make and sell. Think about how you could do them yourself and beat the competition.
6. Keep your ears open. Listen to what people are always saying should be done a little better and smarter. Then figure out how to do it.

START SMALL, THINK BIG

Karen Neidlinger was working as a volunteer at Child Quest International, an organization in San Jose, California that looks for missing kids. Karen spotted a photo of a missing child who turned out to be one of her friends at school. She realized it would be easier to track down missing children if kids their own age were on the lookout for them, so she posted a bulletin board at school. She posted photos of missing kids on her Child Quest Teen Watch board at her high school, along with toll-free numbers to call if anyone spotted a missing child. Karen and her brother are now looking for volunteers at other schools to join them in their effort to find children.

Spotting the Trends for Your Biz Ideas

LEARN

Anything that someone has done before you is a living lesson. That means you can learn from their **mistakes** as well as their successes.

And about those mistakes. You don't have to crash and burn **yourself** in order to know what NOT to do. People are usually happy to share their not-so-successful stories, if only to relive a disaster that they overcame. Ask about the worst workday they ever had, or about the big work blunders that seem funny now when they look back on them.

For example, consider the story of a Girl Boss who was selling knitted scarves and forgot to make sure her yarn was colorfast. The scarves ended up bleeding all over the white t-shirts she sold them with. She may cringe when she tells you about it, but laugh about how she learned from the experience.

CHECKLIST: Here's a List of Places for HOT Information

LOOK

Always keep your eyes peeled for great ideas that you wish you'd thought of yourself. Just because it's already been done doesn't mean you can't do something similar—or better. Plus, once you get into the mindset of thinking like an entrepreneur—of seeing a great idea in the marketplace and making a mental note on how it was done—ideas will start popping into your head for great biz ideas all the time.

Look for ideas that you think are stupid too. Make note of them and check back to see whether they've taken off or whether they've bombed. Why? To test your instincts and develop a sense of what works and what doesn't. That way you can test your judgment without any risk.

"Remember, Ginger Rogers did everything Fred Astaire d

1. Surf through Internet Web sites
2. Browse magazines at the newsstand
3. Observe what other people are reading—go to a coffeehouse or newsstand and check out what seems to interest others
4. Read newsletters from organizations that interest you—non-profits,universities, museums, art galleries, and even bands have newsletters or zines that can keep you informed on what's up.

LISTEN

Listen to what kids at school are saying. Focus on what certain kids—the ones who always seem to be on the cutting edge—think is cool. Become a cool thinker yourself. The more you listen to what everyone else is talking about TODAY, the better you'll be able to predict what they'll talk about TOMORROW. And there's no reason you can't be the Girl Boss in charge of the next hot trend.

Also listen for what ISN'T cool. Keep your ears open for what kids are dissing because it's old or tired. Just because the Gap is selling red nail polish doesn't mean it's cool—especially if no one you know is wearing it. Trust yourself and your friends' opinions before you trust the marketers of big retail chains.

TALK

The more people you talk to the better. Let everyone know you're making clay pencil holders or woven barrettes. The expression "tell a friend" came from Girl Bosses like you who needed to get the word out about what they were doing.

Don't worry about getting your ideas ripped off. By the time you start spreading the word about what you're doing, you'll be so far ahead of the competition that no one will be able to catch you. Plus, with your own signature style, you'll have an individual product that no one can really copy.

Let everyone know where to find you, how to reach you, what you charge, and how willing you are to do the work. No one will know you're there if you just sit at home waiting for the phone to ring. Use every opportunity you have to talk about what you're doing and generate interest.

READ

It may seem like you've got enough to read just getting through your schoolwork. But this is a different kind of reading. Pick up magazines and read about new trends. Decide for yourself whether you think they're such a big deal or not. Look though Internet sites and see what they're saying is hot or cool—make bookmarks for yourself so you can go right to the cool new sites listed by search engines.

Flip through the newspaper—you don't have to read every word—but keep a general eye on the trends in fashion, sports, in small business. Focus especially on any special sections your daily newspaper has devoted to small business owners—many papers offer advice to girl-boss thinkers like you.

ly she did it backwards and in high heels."

—Faith Whittlesey

What's in a Name?

Making it Officia

Names have power.

Think of all the times you've grabbed something off the shelf because the name caught your eye. Don't be fooled—a lot goes into picking a great name, whether it's the name of a product or the name of a business. For example, if you're making painted tea canisters filled with mixtures of homegrown herbal tea, you have some choices. Be creative.

Be Clever

IT'S IMPORTANT TO BE UNIQUE so your product stands out from all the others out there. Calling your product simply "Tea" is not too exciting. True, people will know exactly what it is, but you won't win awards for originality. Think harder.

Your customers will respond to a clever name for your business. Think of ways to play on the theme of drinking tea, pouring tea, going caffeine-free, sitting with a hot cup in your hands. Try some free association games—sit with a piece of paper writing anything that comes into your mind that has to do with tea. Let your mind wander and look at the ideas you've written down when you're finished, not before. Then, for example, you might choose to call your tea something like **Mellow Cup**—it's creative, descriptive and evokes a nice feeling that you'd like to associate with drinking your tea.

Be Clear

BUT DON'T GO OVERBOARD. Sometimes, in the effort to be hip, there's a tendency to forget clarity. Your name shouldn't confuse people. Calling your product **Tea Time** is clear and straightforward. Everyone will know what you're selling. In a busy world, you want people to take a quick glance at a tin of your tea in a display and know exactly what it is. You could even include a description on the packaging. So, for example, if you decided to call your mint-flavored tea **Mystery Mint,** you could write on the packaging that it's mint herbal tea.

MELLOW CUP?

TEA

READING LEAVES?

TEASER?

with the Right Handle

Be Subtle

THINK ABOUT FINDING A NAME that is eye-catching and intriguing enough to make people take a second look. You could call it something like **Reading Leaves,** referring to the Chinese art of reading tea leaves, and also suggesting that your tea might be good to drink while enjoying a good book.

But don't go so far that you actually confuse people. Being **too** clever can backfire and leave people wondering what you're selling. And not everyone on a busy day will take the time to find out. Calling your product **Teaser,** for example, could be downright confusing. If you send out fliers advertising **Teaser,** people will have to read further to figure out what it is. That's not always bad, but you don't want them to walk right past your tea display because they've confused it with tins of cookies.

More Name Challenges

YOU ALSO NEED TO COME UP with a name for your business. This should be fun. If you're going to make fliers or postcards to advertise what you're doing, you can really hook people with a cute or clever name for your business. Don't forget that you can also use your design ability on any fliers, letterhead, or business cards to really get across your message.

If you're doing something artistic, for example, your business name could be your name plus something catchy like **Designs,** or **Crafted by,** or **Homemade.** That way you've personalized your approach by linking your name with that of your business. You can decide whether you want to use your first name or your whole name. Or you can make up a name of some whimsical character who can be your business alias. Why not have some fun?

Your business name can also be descriptive of the kind of work you do. If you run a cooking or catering business, think about including those words in the name. If you make hats, you could use something whimsical like **Mad Hatter,** or come up with something that includes your name or the city where you live: **New York Hats,** for example.

Be Consistent

THE MOST IMPORTANT THING is to pick a name and stick with it. That way your name and the name of your products will begin to build a business identity for you. Of course, when you're just starting out, you can still opt to change it if you come up with something wildly better after only a few weeks. But once you get rolling, you'll want to build name recognition. Your business name will begin to be associated with your skills and your growing success. Keep your business identity so customers will know where to find you.

MAD HATTER?

IME?

MYSTERY MINT?

Your Work Space

Finding the Place to Do Your Thing

Okay, clearly it would be great to rent some cool digs in a glass-walled penthouse to run your business. But save that thought for a little ways down the road—keep a folder, filled with your stellar ideas for the ultimate future office, including tropical fish tanks and vending machines if those are part of the dream. Keep adding ideas to the folder, including magazine pictures of offices that you think are the height of hip, and anything else that will help your dream office become a reality—someday.

In the meantime, you can make a great workspace from what you have. Girl Bosses who are just starting out—or any new business owner for that matter—have the double challenge of conserving resources. That means finding a workspace that isn't too expensive, but still lets your customers know that you mean business. Most start-up businesses begin in the garage—literally. If part of your parents' garage isn't being used for storage or car shelter, ask if you can set up shop there. You could also consider carving out a place for yourself **indoors**—either in a corner of your room or in a guest room that isn't being used full-time.

Once you've staked out your turf and okayed it with the folks, make it your space. Bring all your supplies, folders, to-do lists and other materials you've gathered and organize them in your home office. And don't be misled into thinking that an office needs to be a huge space. One desk drawer in your room may be all you need when you're just starting out.

Once your business begins to grow, you may need to expand. But hold off on your plans to rent expensive space somewhere—find out if a relative has extra room in a spare part of their house. Or if your business is related to what you're doing at school—like tutoring—maybe your school will give you some place where you can work. And if you're working consistently with one or two businesses—selling plant holders to a store for example—find out if you can use some of their office space in exchange for a discount on your prices.

Things to Consider . . .

- **Do you need a large surface to work on?** Consider that an artist probably needs more space to draw and lay out materials than a math tutor needs to correct students' homework.

- **Is the work you're doing going to be messy?** Will you need to work in an area that can get dirty or in a place that can be cleaned up easily?

- **Will you be doing most of your work on a computer?** Will it be more productive for you to move into the computer room in your house? (That is, if you can talk the folks into it.)

- **Does your business require different types of space?** For example, do you need a desk to work on your marketing efforts, a large storage area for supplies, or an area with good ventilation so you don't inhale paint fumes?

- **Will you be making a lot of noise?** Say, recording a demo tape of your music, or hammering stuff together?

The bottom line is that your workspace has to fit your work style. You should feel comfortable working in it, but also motivated to get plenty done. In other words, you don't want to move your home office onto a corner of the couch in front of the T.V., even if it's the most comfortable location in the house. Make sure your workspace is a place where you aren't distracted by noise, friends, or family. This should be fun, but not so fun that you can't be productive!

GREEN THUMBING HER WAY TO GREEN BUCKS

Michelle Tees looked at a ramshackle greenhouse in her family's backyard and saw potential. She did her homework—read books on gardening and learned everything she could about plants. Then she gathered her start-up capital—the money she'd need to launch Michelle's Greenhouses—by working at all kinds of jobs. Eventually she had $3,500 and started fixing up the greenhouse.

Then she grew her business from the ground up—literally. She planted seeds—hundreds of them—and snipped plant clippings from willing neighbors and relatives. She planted everything according to what she'd learned from all her research and gave the seedlings lots of water and attention.

Her business began to bloom and after her first year, she was making a profit. She worked hard—about 20 hours a week—but it has paid off. Michelle has sold more than $30,000 of flowers and plants and secured a tidy profit of more than $10,000. Now she has seven greenhouses, two employees and best of all, she's only just begun. Michelle is 13 years old. If she could harvest such great success, you can too.

Hooking Up and Turning On to the Web

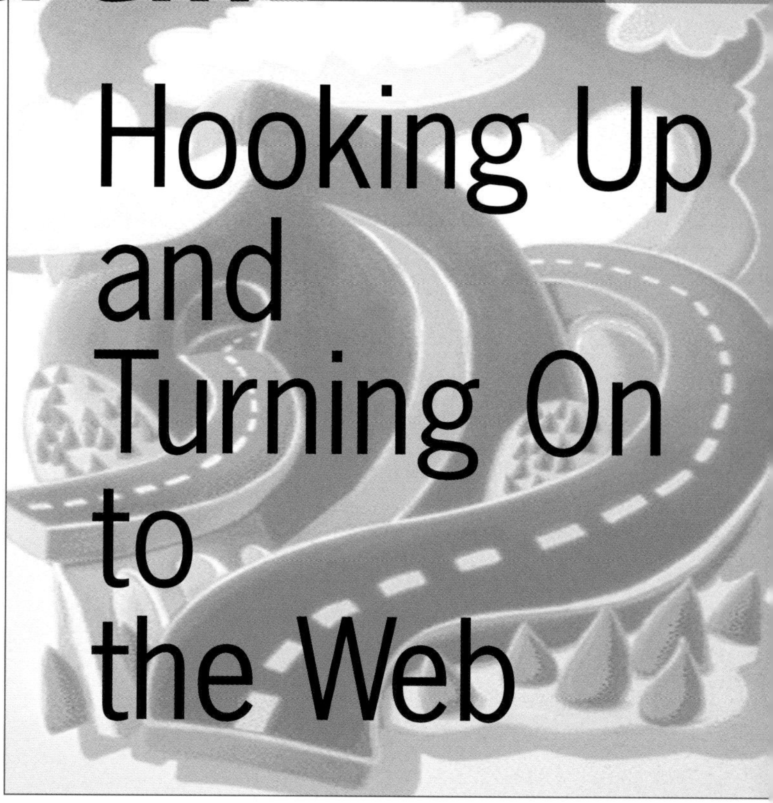

Getting hip to the Web scene is powerful. You can hook up, share ideas, get info, and stay in the worldwide loop by zooming into cyberspace. Consider yourself lucky. The generations of Girl Bosses before you didn't have the kind of cyber possibilities you have today, right at your fingertips: you can get connected through chatrooms, do research by looking at Web sites, keep in touch through e-mail. The possibilities are almost endless, and goddess Girl Boss that you are, you'll take advantage of all of them. Whether you have access to a computer at home, at school, or a relative's house, you can get wired and use it to grow your business. Here's how:

Get Ideas

Use the Internet to gather ideas for the kind of business you want to start. Use search engines to discover all the Web sites that are related to your potential new business: just plug in key words and see what pops up. Look at what other business divas are selling on the Web, and be sure to check out how their Web pages are designed.

You can also scan the Web for ideas about packaging or logos. Take note of Web pages that stand out in your mind—you can use similar techniques in your own packaging or logo design. Also be sure to note what **doesn't** work as well. Sometimes even the most successful businesses make mistakes. Use the very public, very visual medium of the Internet to see the mistakes and successes yourself.

Also keep a list of potential business ideas that you could run online. You might decide to launch a Web magazine or a mail-order company with a Web-based order form. Look for evidence of a similar idea that's already up and running: has your idea already been done, or is there still room for you to fill a niche?

Get the Word Out

The Web is a powerful communications tool. Whether you use chatrooms (for example, girl-rooms where everyone talks about what's cool), or whether you set up your own Web page to publicize your business, the Web is a great way to get noticed. Many Internet service providers—such as Earthlink—let their users put up a free Web page. Take advantage of the opportunity if you already subscribe to one of these services, or if you're considering a new subscription, pick one that allows you to design a Web page for **free**.

Chatrooms are a great place to get feedback on your business questions and find out what other Girl Bosses are doing. Spend some time just listening, checking out what others are saying, and keeping notes. Then jump in with topics you want to discuss. Even without seeing the faces of the other cyber grrls, you can bond with them about your business dilemmas. Who knows?—you may build a great network of friends, or even find new customers!

Get Informed

Have a question about . . . anything? The Web is one of the best sources of information around. And the best part is, it's all in one place at your desk. Many organizations post newsletters and maga-

GO CYBER-WILD—

Other Girl Bosses have done it

* 23% of women business owners have a home page on the Internet, compared to only 16% of male business owners

* 47% of women business owners subscribe to an online service, compared to 40% of men who own businesses

Source: National Foundation of Women Business Owners

CHECK IT OUT

* Get connected: iVillage is a great women's Web site for finding business ideas and financial wisdom— **www.ivillage.com**

* Hook up: with the Young Entrepreneurs Network, a Boston-based consulting company for young business owners— **www.idye.com**

* Look on the Web for biz clues: Directory of Women Business Owners and Professionals at Women's Connection Online— **www.womenconnect.com**

zines on the Internet, free for the taking. You might want to keep a few bookmarks of especially useful sites. For example, if you're running a math tutoring business, you may want to use a statistic in your promotional materials about how many students are barely passing math. You can get this kind of information from government Web sites—the U.S. Department of Labor and the Census Bureau have lots of statistics and charts—and include them in your materials. (Just be sure to credit the source of your information.)

There are also great Web sites for small businesses or home offices—just type in the key words to find them—and they're updated all the time. They have question and answer sections and useful tips to help you run your start-up more efficiently. Learn from the experience of other diva bosses—many have advice columns just for girls like you!

Ms. Foundation for Women

TAKE OUR DAUGHTERS TO WORK®

Take Our Daughters to Work® Day *is a great way to start thinking about the kind of business you'd like to run. It was started in 1993 by the Ms. Foundation for Women, and now takes place every fourth Thursday in April. It's intended to give girls a window to the real working world by encouraging them to go to work with a family member or friend. Think about the people you know with cool jobs—it could be a parent, neighbor, or friend. This could be your chance to find out what they really do!*

Marie Wilson (the president of the Ms. Foundation for Women) receives hundreds of letters each year from girls who want to spend the day with their favorite lady bosses. The Ms. Foundation for Women has made many of those dreams come true. In 1998, hundreds of girls got to visit the United Nations in New York, for example. (There they rubbed elbows with the first woman deputy secretary general—a real diva boss.) Across the country, in Los Angeles, another group of girls visited Twentieth Century-Fox for a studio tour.

What to Do

Find someone who has a job that really interests you. Think about what you know about your parents' jobs. If you don't really understand what they do all day, this could be your chance to find out. But if you've already been to your parents' offices, you might want to pick someone else as your mentor for the day. If you have a friend of the family who works for a wildlife preservation institute or a neighbor who directs television commercials, maybe you'd rather spend the day with them! And don't be too shy to ask—they won't know you're interested unless you speak up.

Or, take a completely different tack. Find someone with a job you know absolutely nothing about. You'd be surprised at what can become exciting once you've gone behind the scenes. Maybe you have a relative who works for an aerospace company—do you have any idea what people actually do there? Use the day to find out!

For more information on Take Our Daughters to Work® Day, check out their web site at www.ms.foundation.org or call 1-800-676-7780

Alexandra Desaulniers was a Girl Boss in the making when she wrote a letter to President Clinton asking if she could come to work with him on **Take Our Daughters to Work® Day.**

She also wrote to Marie Wilson, president of the Ms. Foundation for Women, to express how much she wanted to see the country's biggest decision makers in action. Alexandra ultimately wasn't able to spend the day at the White House, but she had a great experience and corresponded with several top government officials.

Alexandra E. Desaulniers

President William J. Clinton
The White House
1600 Pennsylvania Avenue
Washington, D.C. 20500

Dear Mr. Clinton,

Last week was my first trip to Washington, D.C. and it was very exciting! I got to see all the monuments, the Smithsonian, and the Capitol. I even got to see you! I was walking back to our hotel with my Mom and Dad, last Tuesday, February 18th. You were coming home and waved to me from your car.

When I grow up, I am going to be the President of the United States, too! I think it's a really neat job, even though it's hard work. I like work, it's my favorite word. I work hard in school and get straight A's. I also like to swim on my swim team and rollerblade. Does the White House have a swimming pool? Do you know how to rollerblade? I can teach you! It's easy and lots of fun!!

Anyway, this April 24th is Annual Take Our Daughters To Work Day, and I would like to go to work with you for the day. I think that would be a great way to find out more about my future job. Please call me right away, so I can let my teacher know that I will not be in school that day. I get home around 6:30 p.m. after swim team practice.

I can't wait to meet you! Maybe we can rollerblade at lunchtime. I have extra knee and elbow pads that you can borrow.

Sincerely,

Alex Desaulniers

Alexandra E. Desaulniers

THE WHITE HOUSE
WASHINGTON

Dear Alexandra,

Thanks so much for asking to speak with me in person. I always enjoy meeting with young people from all over our country, and I'm sorry that my busy schedule prevented me from meeting with you. Maybe someday we'll have an opportunity to visit.

I encourage you to continue setting high goals for the future. By working hard in school and standing up for your beliefs, you are preparing for the time when your generation will be leading America in the 21st century.

Best wishes for every future success.

Sincerely,

Bill Clinton

Web Sites for Women-Owned Business Organizations

African-American Women Entrepreneurs	http://www.aawe.org
Asian Women in Business	http://awib.org
Black Women On the Web	http://www.bwow.com
National Association of Women Business Owners	http://www.nawbo.org
National Foundation for Women Business Owners	http://www.nfwbo.org
Professional Women's Business Exchange	http://www.bayareabiz.com
Women's Business Network	http://www.womenbiz.net
Western Reserve Business Center for Women	http://www.wrbsw.org
Women Business Owners of Manitoba, with chapters in Brandon, Dauphin, Portage, and Winnipeg	http://www.wbom.mb.ca
Women Business Owners of Southeastern Michigan	http://www.wobo.org
Women's Business Ownership	http://www.sbaonline.sba.gov

SECTION 3

Ideas for Your Biz

Get Hip to the Cause—

Businesses That Make a Difference

The food for thought that fuels your own business can be food for others too. Literally. You may have a great idea to start a meals-on-wheels business where you deliver food to people who can't leave their homes. That's a great way to help others AND start a business.

Think about how to combine your Girl Boss instincts with a thriving business. There's almost no end to the ways you can start businesses with a socially responsible twist. Here are a few examples:

Look for opportunities to run individual projects for organizations. Offer to organize a bike ride or a dance-a-thon to raise money for your favorite charity. You may even find that the charity is willing to give you a stipend to run the program. Think about environmental clean-up efforts, local chapters of charities, and even schools in your area who need your help!

PEANUTS reprinted by permission of United Media Syndicate, Inc.

Wendy Kopp started Teach for America during her junior year in college. She looked around and noticed how heavily college students were being recruited for prestigious investment banking jobs, but that there was no similar prestige attached to teaching jobs. She started Teach for America to aggressively recruit great teachers and make it a higher-status profession. What began as a thesis topic became a nationwide organization after Wendy wrote a proposal for her business plan and sent it to chief executive officers of some big companies. She convinced them to fund her start-up and learned as she went along. Today there are hundreds of college graduates in the Teach for America program each year.

Don't Be Afraid To Be Too Idealistic

When you're pursuing a philanthropic business opportunity, don't be afraid to think from the heart. There's no reason why a business that's good for others can't be fun for everyone involved. Think about organizing a car wash for charity. The not-for-profit world is filled with great businesses that raise money for a good cause. They can even provide a fun weekend for their Girl Boss leaders.

Think about starting a beach clean-up day for a local area that really needs it. You might want to start by signing up with a local environmental group that holds events like this to see how they're done. Use the opportunity to meet people and collect names of interested volunteers you can contact for your event.

Your best resource for organizing your own environmental effort is any group that has done it already. Look through the newspaper for similar weekend events and join up. Getting involved will give you an overview of who's doing what in your area and help you spot other important tasks that need to be tackled.

For example, suppose most of your neighbors have fireplaces. You see a nearby lot where workers are clearing away trees to make room for a new house. This is when a Girl Boss gets active! Ask what they plan to do with the trees. If they're just going to end up in a landfill, you could have a philanthropic opportunity on your hands.

See if the workers would be willing to cut the tree trunks and branches into small pieces. Then ask a friend with a car if he will help you haul the wood back to a place where you can sell it as firewood. Be sure to put some newspaper down in the car first—you don't want do make a huge mess, especially when someone is doing you the favor of giving you trunk space for the wood. Also wear gloves so you don't end up with a handful of splinters.

Once you've got the wood piled up, make fliers and take them around to your neighbors, telling them where to come for some great firewood at a good price. You've got yourself a business!

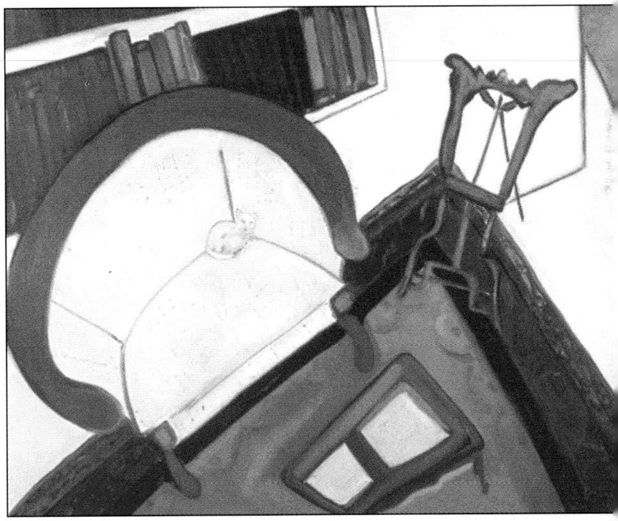

Afraid because it's never been done before? Don't be!

Real Girl Bosses MAKE things happen before anyone else even thinks of it.

Get Informed

Next you need to get hooked into the information pipeline (there is still one beyond the Internet)—get yourself onto mailing lists of local groups that take on the kinds of projects that interest you. If you're into environmental causes, check with organizations like the Sierra Club, the Audubon Society, or Heal the Bay. Or if you're interested in helping the ailing, why not approach a local hospital to see if they'd be interested in you recruiting a group of candy stripers for them. (They might even throw in a free lunch, or give you a jump on a future job opportunity.)

Another idea is to organize a food drive or dance-a-thon for a local charity—the work you do might be unpaid at first, but after you develop it, you have a good chance of being hired to organize another event. That's how the AIDS Ride got started and now it has a huge paid staff running events.

These groups will be happy to let you organize an event to benefit them. They may even offer you resources, like lists of potential volunteers or supplies you may need. They'll also help you avoid certain pitfalls and learn from their experience. Most importantly, they know the process—including how to get local permits—so you will have someone overseeing you and making sure you're doing everything by the book. Why risk it?

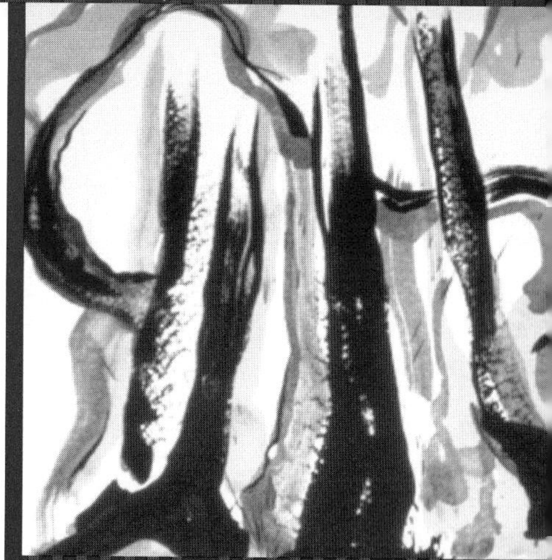

Low Cash Flow

These more philanthropic businesses probably won't make your rich—so don't expect to end up with a wad of cash. But they ARE valuable. The feeling you'll get after a long day of working hard on something you believe in will be its own reward.

And often businesses that start off as purely philanthropic efforts grow into companies that can employ you and a staff of assistants. Look at what happened for Wendy Kopp and her Teach for America concept. Don't let the lack of cash stop you from undertaking a great effort for a good cause. You never know where it might lead!

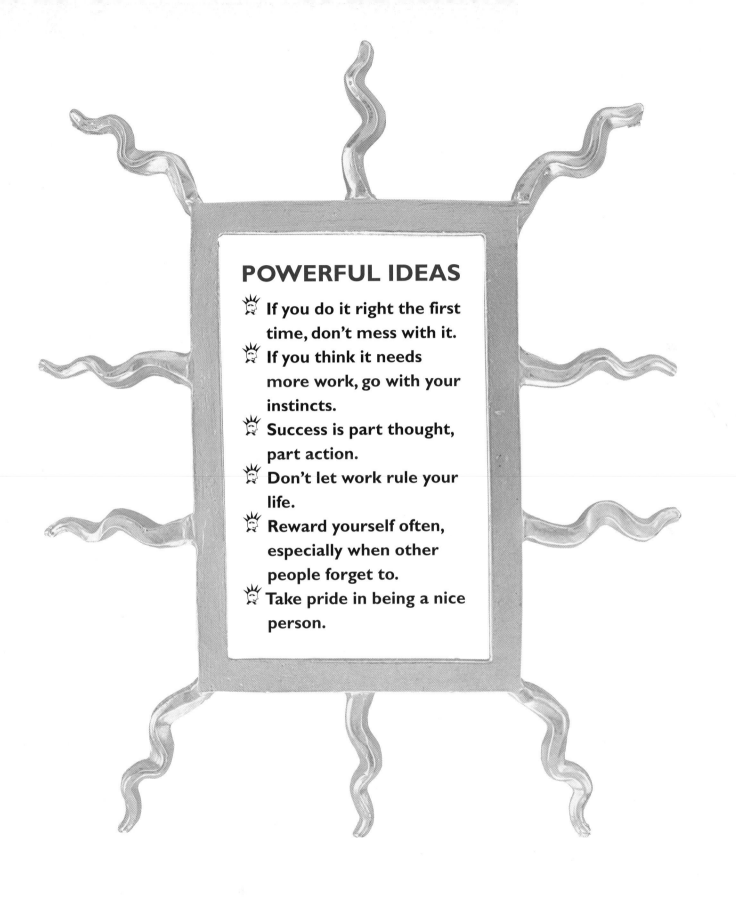

POWERFUL IDEAS

- If you do it right the first time, don't mess with it.
- If you think it needs more work, go with your instincts.
- Success is part thought, part action.
- Don't let work rule your life.
- Reward yourself often, especially when other people forget to.
- Take pride in being a nice person.

Use Your Creative Instincts to Build a Business

When you use your artistic talent to start a business, you're putting your signature touch on everything you sell—that can be a tremendous asset because no imitator will be able to do it in exactly the same way. You'll have the power to develop your own unique brand through your work. The most striking examples of Gir Bosses who have done just that are women in the fashion industry. Women like Coco Chanel or Donna Karan have developed their own lines of clothes that can't be imitated. They've created a brand cache that goes with having their names on all the clothes they make. You can do that too. Start small, think big!

First decide which artistic talent you want to use. Evaluate your abilities and decide whether you have a great photographic eye, whether you are skilled at copying designs onto paper or objects, or whether you have a terrific ability to create original art. Then decide how you want to use your talent in business. Do you want to work with paint, pens, fabric, or beads and wires? Make a few trips to hobby shops, art supply stores, and craft centers to see what kinds of supplies you want to start with, and what they cost.

TRIAL and ERROR

You may try a few different kinds of products before deciding on a business. Experiment with different fabrics, paints, collage combinations and see which is easiest for you to make—and the most fun! Decide which looks best and which will require least supplies. Don't forget that you can always expand later—you may start with painted note cards for now, and expand later into notebooks and t-shirts.

Don't worry if your initial idea doesn't pan out. You might start by stenciling letters onto a t-shirt, but then decide that you'd rather paint freehand. You can always let your business evolve, including new products and new ways of presenting them. The point is to pick a starting place and **get moving.**

And that's the great thing about using art supplies—you often can take something you've made and turn it into something else. Suppose you've dyed a bunch of fabric thinking you'd make sarong skirts, but then decided sarongs aren't going to sell during the winter. You could take the fabric and use it to cover notebooks. Then you could decorate them with beads and sequins and sell them as designer journals. Be creative!

SEE HOW EASY IT IS *Step by Step!* 1

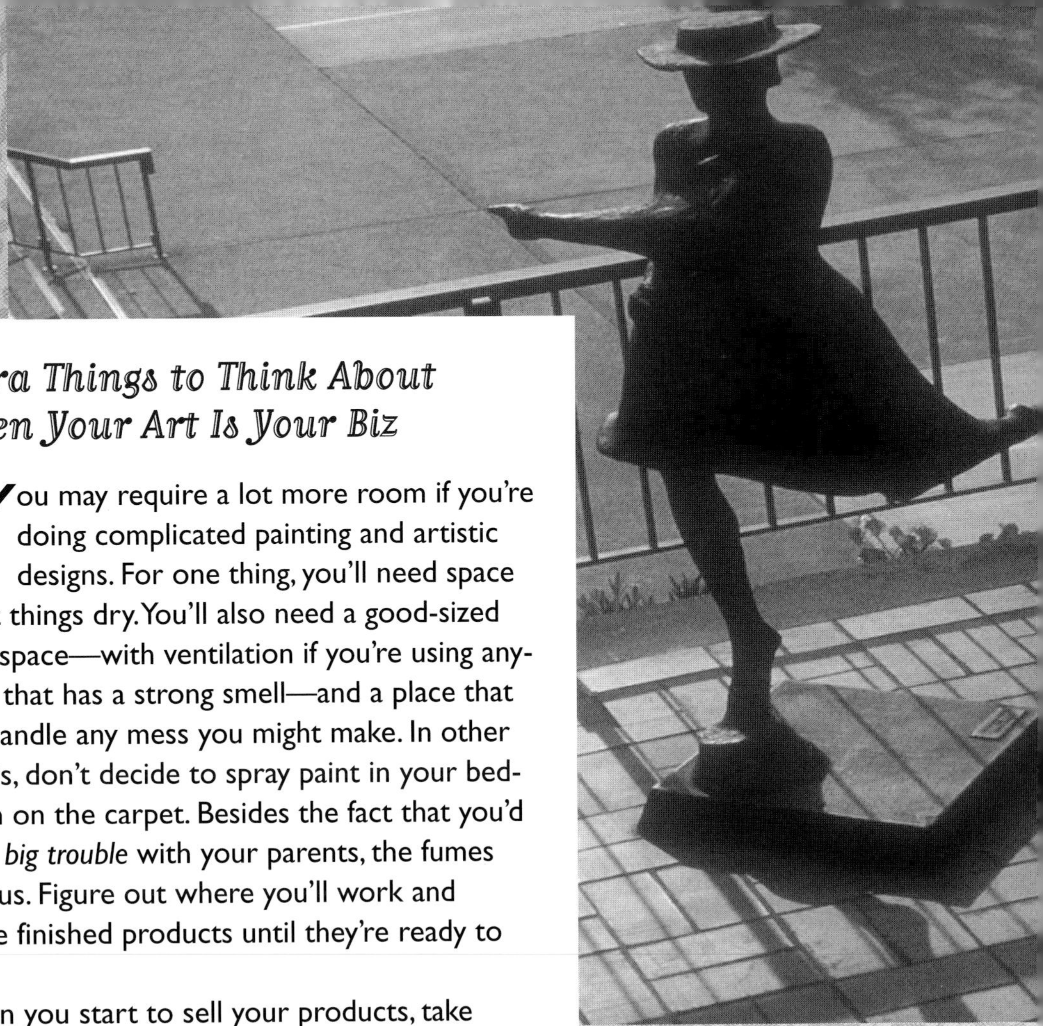

Ideas for Artistic Businesses that Stem from Your Own Talent

- Stenciled, painted, or collage note cards
- Decorated notebooks of lined paper
- Painted clothing, backpacks, purses, scarves, hats
- Jewelry and hair accessories
- Calligraphy services for invitations
- Photography services at parties and events
- Handmade clothing
- Decorated "functional" art, like painted flowerpots or mirrors with mosaic tile borders

Extra Things to Think About When Your Art Is Your Biz

You may require a lot more room if you're doing complicated painting and artistic designs. For one thing, you'll need space to let things dry. You'll also need a good-sized workspace—with ventilation if you're using anything that has a strong smell—and a place that can handle any mess you might make. In other words, don't decide to spray paint in your bedroom on the carpet. Besides the fact that you'd be in *big trouble* with your parents, the fumes could be dangerous. Figure out where you'll work and where you'll store finished products until they're ready to be sold.

Then when you start to sell your products, take advantage of your artistic talent and design great packaging and promotional materials. Get creative with the ways you'll package or display your wares: if you're selling jewelry, for example, decorate cute tags to hang from each piece, showing the name of your business and an inspired logo. Even a simple, well-designed logo is eye-catching and will give your jewelry added appeal to customers. Use your creativity to your advantage!

Signs You've Got a Future as an Artistic Girl Boss

- You love to draw or paint on anything in sight and don't consider it work
- You've gotten compliments on accessories or clothing you've designed yourself
- When you see accessories or jewelry in the store, you always think, *I could do that—in fact, I could make something even better.*
- All of your hobbies are artistic
- You love to spend time browsing at craft stores and art supply stores

MOVIE LADY BOSS

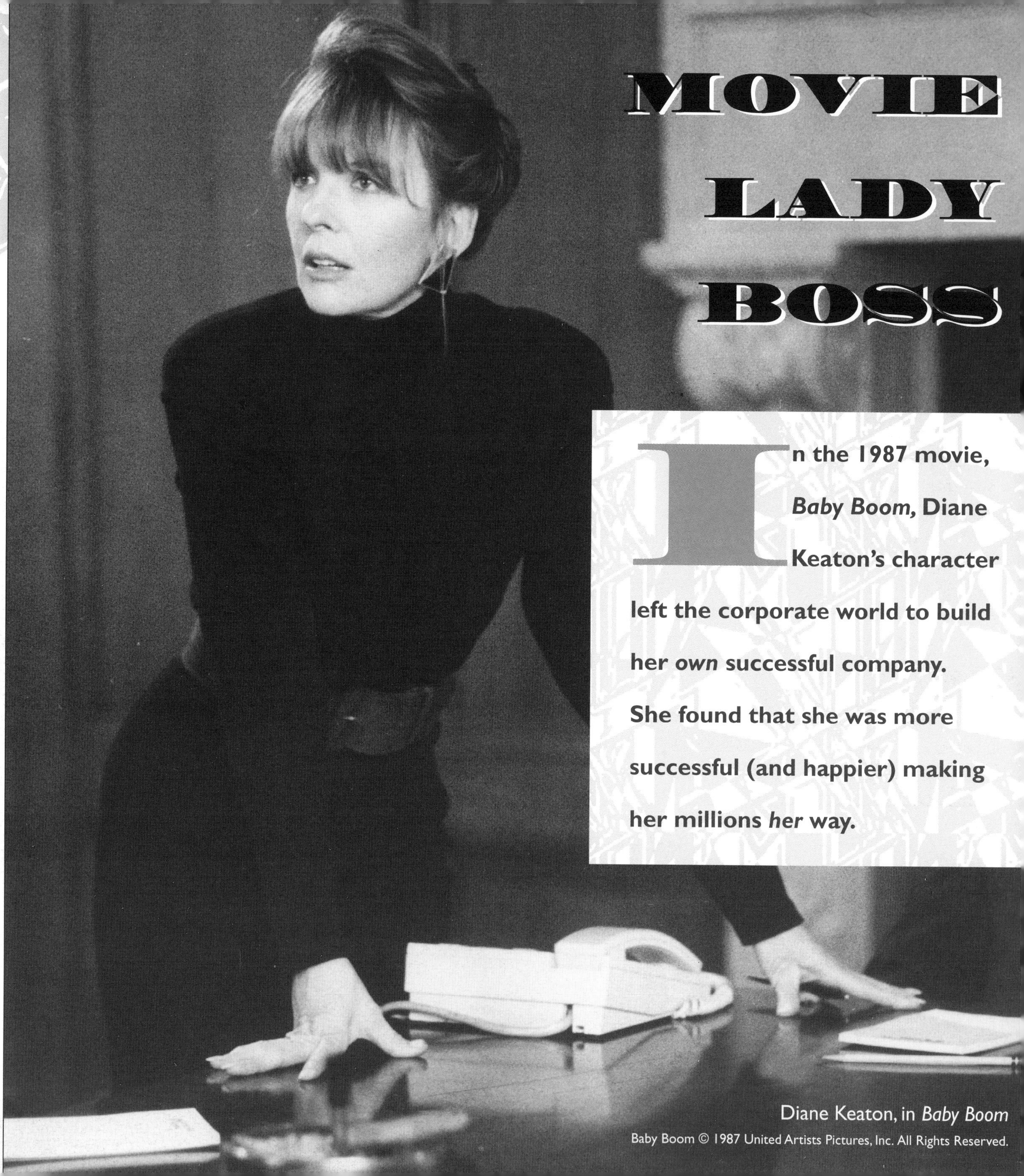

In the 1987 movie, *Baby Boom,* Diane Keaton's character left the corporate world to build her *own* successful company. She found that she was more successful (and happier) making her millions *her* way.

Diane Keaton, in *Baby Boom*

When **Monica Sedillo** isn't playing basketball or baby sitting, she's busy running her vending machine business. She figured out that you don't have to buy a lot of expensive equipment to start a business. When she was 10, Monica saw a business opportunity when her aunt, who's in the vending machine business, offered her an extra machine. Monica bought the double-snack machine, figuring she could fill each side with different snacks and sell them for a profit. The diva boss started thinking about where she could sell snacks from the machine and immediately thought of her school. But in order to launch a serious business, Monica needed to be taken seriously. She outlined her sales plan for the school and promised to sell only healthy snacks. The school agreed and the machines were so successful in her 5th grade class that other teachers started requesting machines to use for fund-raising projects. Last year, Monica bought two more vending machine stands and hired her sisters to service the machines. They get a percentage of the profits.

Now her vending machine generates a profit on every handful her classmates eat. She spends about a nickel for each serving of Boston Baked Beans, peanuts, and other healthy munchies that she sells through the machines and charges a quarter for each serving. So far she's made $1,540 and kept $385 profit after donating $385 to her school.

Monica's advice to Girl Bosses:

"Set a goal and go for it."

Pamela Kuemmerle and Olivia Sellke

Pamela and Olivia's business began as a Beanie Baby collection, not as a business. But the two friends, who are now 12, decided that their animal-shaped bean bags needed sleeping bags. Once they'd made a couple from some extra fabric their parents supplied, they found there was a big demand, just among friends at school. So Pamela and Olivia went to work on their business, In the Bag. Over the past two years they've made dozens of sleeping bags and hundreds of dollars. They let their customers pick the fabric for the Beanie bags and they under-price all the stores in town who sell sleeping bags for Beanies.

Ideas for How to Turn Your Talent into a COOL BIZ

> Resolved—to take fate by the throat and shake a living out of her.
>
> —Louisa May Alcott, *Journal*

Photography

Are you a shutterbug? If you have a flair for taking cool pictures but need a way to get noticed by potential customers, try teaming up with existing stores (but not photo stores, since they're your competition). Go to shops with window displays they might like to jazz up, for example. Think creatively. Approach a pet shop and ask if they'd like you to take pictures of the dogs and cats they're trying to sell. They could post the photographs in their windows, where potential pet-owners could see them without even coming in. Be sure to include your signature at the bottom of each photo, as well as your contact info in case these shoppers need a photographer.

As long as you're at the pet shop, why not ask the owners if they'd like to offer a promotional service for all customers who buy new pets? They could have their picture taken with their new pet on a Saturday at the store. That way the customer gets a little extra something special—especially if they've bought a new puppy or kitten which will grow bigger by the day—and the store owners might get new business and keep their customers happy. And you'll get a commission for each photo you take!

Always look for opportunities where everyone benefits and you'll have a slam-dunk biz opportunity.

Can You Hold a Tune?

Think about all the places where music is welcome. Restaurants often hire piano players during dinner, or department stores often want acappella groups to sing—all to attract customers. Contact shopping malls or individual stores if you've got a group of singers or musicians who will entertain during holidays or weekends. You'll be surprised at how willing people will be to support your efforts. And don't be surprised if you and your talented group of singers are booked for weeks at a time—better hurry up and pick a name for your group. The Girl Divas?

If you play an instrument like the piano really well, consider playing at parties. No, not the kind of ragers you and your friends want to have—the kind of parties your parents and **their** friends have. And, if you're really good, don't be afraid to charge full fare for an evening's entertainment.

Start with people you know. If your parents' friends are having a dinner party, they'd be crazy not to want a little live entertainment in the background. Everyone at the party will hear you play, so don't be surprised if you get a few calls afterward asking you to play at another event. They may even tell other friends about you. Don't underestimate the power of word of mouth. That's how you build a business.

Girl Boss Rule

GET EXPERIENCE NOW

It's never too soon to start getting the experience that will help you run your own business. Interning is a great way to begin. You have the advantage of a built-in mentor and a built-in school tailored to your field. People are always looking for enthusiastic workers to start at the bottom. The great thing about internships is that you can almost always find someone who's willing to let you help out. This is partly because interns generally don't get paid, so it doesn't take much to convince someone to let you work for her. And the education and experience you'll get is worth it.

Internships come in all shapes and sizes. Sometimes the newer the company, the more you'll get to do. You could ask to work at a start-up internet company, for example, and end up with tons of responsibility because everyone who works there pulls an equal share. At an established law firm, on the other hand, you could end up with little more than plant-watering responsibilities. Sometimes you can have more of an apprenticeship, which essentially means you're working for one person to learn their business. Artists, musicians, architects, and other creative professionals provide good opportunities to work one-on-one and learn an art or a trade.

When you start, just make sure you know what to expect—long hours, driving on the job, errand running—and also make sure the people you're working for know what you can do. If you're a genius on the computer, make sure your boss knows it—you'll probably be given more interesting stuff to do and will get a better experience out of your internship.

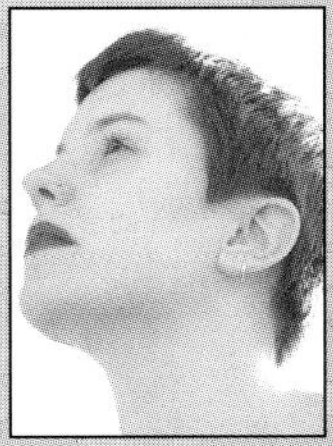

Use Your Head

If you're a whiz at something like math or writing, use it as the anchor for a hot business. Tutors can make the big bucks! Don't take your school smarts for granted—not everyone has them. Just because geometry comes easily to you doesn't mean all the other kids feel the same way.

You don't have to teach or tutor your friends. That could get awkward. But kids who are a few years younger are the perfect candidates for your tutoring services. Plus, if you tutor kids who go to the same school as you, you could have the advantage of knowing the coursework since you've already studied it.

If you work as a tutor, sometimes your school can help you find students who need your help. They'll know the most about who may need it. One big benefit of working through your school is that often you can do the tutoring right on campus—either after school or during your lunch break. So you can fit it into your schedule before you even go home for the day. Not bad—making some extra money and still having some free time left over after school. Of course, once word gets out that you're the tutor extraordinaire, you'll be so busy you'll barely be able to fit everyone in. But that's one of the great problems that every good Girl Boss has to face.

Be Artistic

Paint, draw, or stencil your way to a successful business. If you have artistic talent, chances are your friends know it. When kids know you've got a flair with a paintbrush or pen, almost anything you write or draw becomes a piece of artwork to them.

Think about what you can paint or draw on: terra cotta flower pots, coffee mugs, glass bottles, t-shirts, jeans, tennis shoes, backpacks—the possibilities are almost endless. You can create all kinds of wonderful designs. And even if you're not a born artist, you can still be creative. You can use stencils or stamp prints onto fabric—or even use kits from craft stores to create printed fabric to sew into skirts or fold into scarves. That's how the pros do it.

The bottom line is, if you make something that looks good and has a **purpose**—like clothing or a painted piece of furniture—you'll have a much easier time making a sale. If you can create functional or wearable art, you'll find people to buy everything you make. Just watch!

Be a Pioneer—Finding Uncharted Territory

Some pioneering ideas never existed before their entrepreneurial Girl Bosses came up with them. Indie Power came from Girl Bosses who thought big and figured out ways to make small independent companies grow from a tiny idea. You can be the same kind of leader!

A lot of great business ideas start with, well, **ideas.** Think about all those days you went shopping, looking for a magazine with the kinds of articles you wanted to read or looking for the kind of clothes that fit your style. If you're looking for something that doesn't exist, figure out if you can make it **yourself.**

Also, listen to people around you. If you fashioned a skirt out of a big scarf you found at a western museum and everyone is raving about it, you may be onto a new style of clothes. If people like your new ideas, you could be in business!

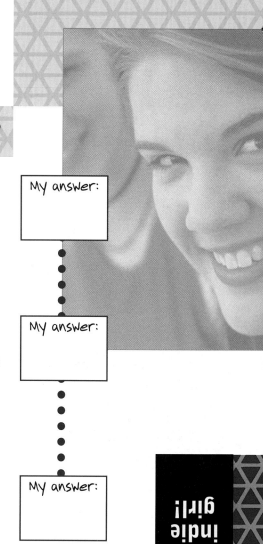

QUIZ—Do You Have Indie Power?

1 **You're walking through a shop and see a case full of bracelets that look like plastic fishtank tubing with different beads inside. Do you:**

A Buy one, hoping they'll be all the rage in a few weeks?

B Look closer and figure out how it's put together and become the first in your school to sell them?

C Decide they're ugly because they look like fishtank tubing?

My answer:

2 **You're looking at zines and wonder why no one has ever come out with one that gives updates on the wake boarding scene. Do you:**

A Write an e-mail to a sports-related zine and ask them to feature some wake boarding in the future?

B Write to a sports-related zine and offer to write about wake boarding for them?

C Decide that wake boarding must not be all that cool if none of the zines feature anything about it?

My answer:

3 **You've been playing acoustic guitar for years and everyone has been telling you how good you sound. Do you:**

A Offer to give free lessons?

B Make a demo tape and try sending it out to radio stations and record labels?

C Buy lottery tickets and hope you'll win enough money to cut a record?

My answer:

Answers: B an indie girl!

No one ever wore baby blue nail polish before **Dineh Mohajer**'s company Hard Candy came along. And if she hadn't had faith in her own ideas, no one would ever have heard of her company. Dineh was mixing up her own wild nail polish colors because none of the ones out there were interesting enough. She made the first batches of nail polish in her kitchen. Sure enough, people started asking where she got the polish and Dineh realized she was onto a great business idea. Now her business is growing fast and has been written up in all kinds of newspapers and magazines. She saw a need for something that didn't exist and filled it herself. So can you!

Look at indie magazines, Web pages and zines for ideas about indie businesses or creative concepts you can pursue. If you think it's a good idea and it doesn't exist, maybe it should!

Define Indie

Fortunately, you have a lot to work with—there is a whole world of ideas just waiting to become full-fledged businesses.

Great girl musicians have been on the rise lately and we love that! But none of them waited until there was a wave of girl bands before they picked up an instrument or wrote a song. Jewel, Brandy, and Alanis Morrisette were all writing songs and singing long before their careers took off. And no one could guarantee them that they would be stars someday—they had to move ahead with their music anyway. They had to get out **in front** of the trend so they could be ready when it was their time under the spotlight.

That's what being an indie girl means. It means being ahead of what's happening now and creating the next big thing. In part, you've got to love what you're doing. But you've also just got to do it. You've got to work on it, sing, dance, play the guitar—whatever—until you're so good that the world has no other choice but to hear you.

That's indie power.

SPACE PIONEER: SALLY RIDE

Sally Ride was the first U.S. woman in space, flying on the orbiter *Challenger* in 1983. It took more than a love of adventure to become an astronaut—Sally was a first-class physicist when she was selected for training.

Trade Magazine Resources

NONPROFIT BIZ

Recycling Today Magazine

Water Conditioning and Purifying Magazine Online

Fund$Raiser Cyberzine

APPAREL

Clothing BIZ

Apparel Strategist

California Apparel News

Women's Wear Daily

Textile World

ART

Art Talk

Craft Supply Magazine

JEWELRY

National Jeweler

Orchid Digest

Lapidary Journal

Modern Jeweler

Ornament

Metalsmith

CRAFTS

Fine Woodworking

Furniture World Magazine

Lawn and Landscape Magazine

Handcraft

COMPUTERS

Computer User

MicroDesign Resources

MMWire

New Computer News

Software News

TechWeek

COSMETICS

Cosmetics and Toiletries

Happi Magazine

SECTION 4

Getting the Word Out

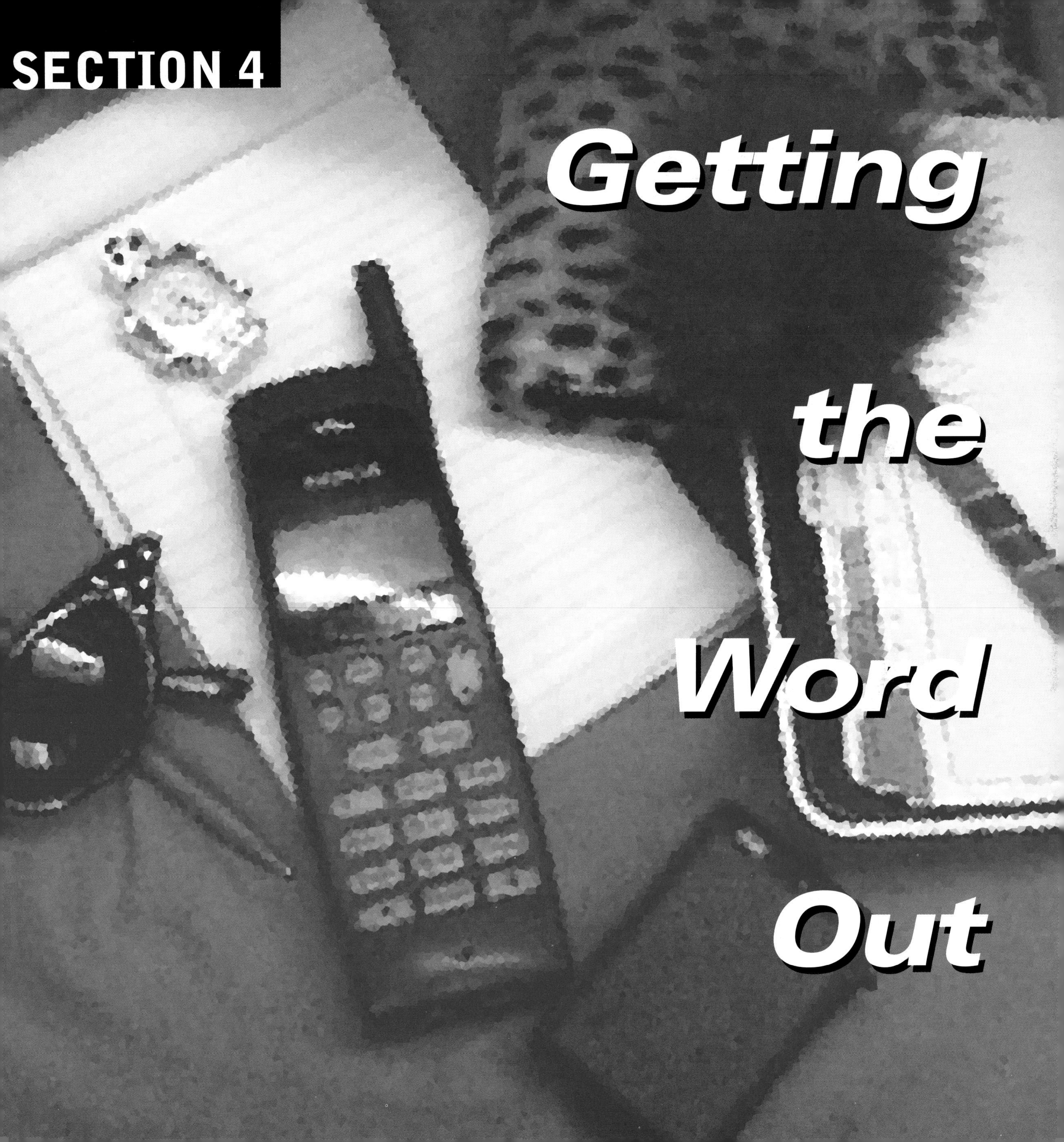

How to Let the World Know You're Here

If you're going to make your mark, you need an identity. You need it all: business cards, letterhead, promotional materials, fliers—but don't worry. They're all easy to make on your personal computer. (If you don't have a PC, ask your favorite teacher how you can use the resources at school.) You can use simple graphics programs to design letterhead and matching business cards. Print out the business cards on heavier paper and cut them apart using a paper cutter.

The bottom line is, no matter how great your idea is, it can't go anywhere if no one knows about it. There are all kinds of fancy names for people who come up with ways to get attention: publicists, advertisers, public relations specialists. What they all essentially do, in different ways and for different types of clients, is get attention for a person, a company, or a product by coming up with catchy "hooks." Bigger companies hire outside promotions experts, but when you're just starting out, there's a lot you can do for yourself.

There is a whole industry based on this kind of promotional work. Businesses pay tens of thousands of dollars in the hope that their products will get the attention of future customers. But you don't need to hire an expensive firm to promote your business—at least not when you're starting out. There are plenty of ways to do your own promotions.

Coco was one of the first real lady bosses of the century. She opened her own shop in 1912 to design clothes, and was all the rage by 1920. Her perfume, Chanel No. 5, is still one of the most popular in the world.

Coco Chanel
Fashion Pioneer

> ***How many cares one loses when one decides not to be something, but to be someone.***
>
> —COCO CHANEL, ***Fashion Designer***

Consider posting fliers with "tear-off" slips at the bottom to advertise your services. People can simply tear off your phone number and call you. Post them around your neighborhood, at schools or gyms, or near busy business districts with a lot of foot traffic. (Just be sure you ask permission before you post one in a privately-owned business.)

Don't forget to make your fliers eye-catching. People have to notice them before they'll start reading them. If your flier looks like just another advertisement, it won't get anyone's attention. Think about going with color (try to get a good deal on color xeroxing)—that will make those fliers really vivid.

You also can send out a printed postcard to people you think are likely customers. For example, if you're making jewelry, you might target small clothing stores that have jewelry departments, showing a picture of your designs and providing a contact phone number. Or if you're offering tutoring services, why not target your mailing to schools in your area, or hand them out after school to parents?

Don't forget to get postcard stamps from the post office, or better yet—pre-stamped postcards that you can draw on yourself and then mail. Both are cheaper than the cost of a regular stamp—don't get caught putting regular letter-rate stamps on postcards. (Every penny counts.) And like your fliers, make your postcards stand out. You don't have to foot the bill for color copying—try printing them on colored paper instead. That way they'll stand out from the regular mail.

Good Ideas, Bad Ideas:
Decide which ones are which

1. **Go around town and tear off other people's fliers and throw them away. That way yours will stand out.**
2. **Offer to give your first 20 customers a free gift.**
3. **Empty out your savings account to take out an ad in the newspaper for your new business.**
4. **Print up expensive sweatshirts to advertise your product and ask your friends to wear them.**
5. **Print up inexpensive colorful bookmarks that advertise your product and give them away.**

Answers

1. No. Even in business, you need to play fair. Besides, if you rip off other people's fliers, what will stop them from returning the favor?

2. Yes. Free gifts are a good incentive that will encourage people to buy from you sooner rather than later.

3. No. Big ads like these are too expensive and come with no guarantee that they'll work.

4. No. Again, this is too expensive. And people might not want to serve as walking billboards for you!

5. Yes. Small items like bookmarks are a great low-cost way to advertise to lots of people.

DON'T SPIN OUT OF CONTROL

Publicity is a basic reality of the business world. There are so many companies out there, each with a different product or idea that is "better" than the next company's. They're all trying to get across the idea that theirs is the best.

Of course, companies with big publicity budgets don't stop at sending out fliers. A dog food company, for example, might send out free samples to pet owners, or even send a dog food dish as a free gift. If you look around, you'll notice all kinds of free gifts, coupons, mail-in rebates, food samples—you name it.

The problem is, these tactics all cost money—lots of it. When you're just starting out, don't feel the need to compete with big established players with huge budgets. Go at your own pace. Keep an eye on what they do and store it away in your memory bank. But keep your promotions on a scale that's consistent with a start-up. And remember the credo: start small, think big.

Girl Boss Rule

Be Honest

Honesty is such a basic tenet of the Girl Boss code that it almost needs no mention. **Almost.** But then there's temptation. You're collecting commissions from a restaurant that hired you to go from table to table playing the violin, and you're handed twice as much as you know you've earned. The restaurant manager hasn't been paying attention and thinks you've played at more tables than you have. The honest—and right—thing to do is to explain the miscalculation and take the money you deserve. The restaurant manager, and the owners, will appreciate your honesty and more than likely send you more business because of it. An honest Girl Boss is one they'll want to do business with.

Remember, though, that you're not required to tell people things just because they ask. Being honest doesn't mean you have to tell your competitor how much money you're making. You can keep your professional secrets without being dishonest. And you're not required to tell a future customer how much you charged the last customer. You're entitled to raise your prices if it's the right time to do so, and if someone bullies you into coughing up too much information, you might lose out on profits you rightfully deserve.

One other unfortunate truth, however, is that people may not always be honest with *you*. Don't believe everything you hear. The business world can be quite cut-throat at times. Just because the guy who's trying to sell you a leather jacket tells you the original price is three times the "special" price he's charging you doesn't make it true. So be wary when something seems too good to be true. But when it's your turn to sell, do it honestly. Your business will be better off because of it.

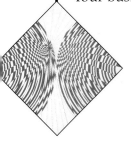

Aura Dimon was having a hard time finding the hippest fashions in the department stores in her New York neighborhood. So the 18-year-old Girl Boss began making her own clothes and started a trend in the process. When she started her clothing line, Auraze, including rave pants with a 60-inch flare, Bloomingdale's took notice and featured her pants in their New York City store windows. Now they're in even more stores and her clothing line is expanding to include tops and new fabrics. She even started her own Web site to sell her designs at www.auraze.com.

The New WNBA
A League of Their Own

(l to r):
Teresa Weatherspoon, New York Liberty;
Michelle Edwards, Cleveland Rockers;
Sheryl Swoopes, Houston Comets;
Lisa Leslie, Los Angeles Sparks;
Nikki McCray, Washington Mystics;
Tina Thompson, Houston Comets;
Andrea Stinson, Charlotte Sting;
Michele Timms, Phoenix Mercury

Profile

Jamila Wideman, guard for the LA Sparks and the WNBA's Girl Boss of the courts, has been playing basketball for as long as she can remember. She played with her dad and two older brothers and bucked convention to attend an all-boys sports camp every summer—she was the only girl. She knew that if opportunities existed, she needed to take advantage of them, even if they were supposed to be for boys only.

"On the first day, no one would want me on their team. But then I got on the court and played. The next day, everyone wanted me on their team. It mattered more that I could play."

Jamila says her hometown, which had no basketball teams for girls when she was growing up, now has two girls' teams and is considering a third. Jamila herself coaches clinics for kids with basketball dreams, hoping to encourage them to keep playing. She started a program called "Hoopin with Jamila" to teach kids basketball and some reading and writing. "They've been craving opportunity—to get close to someone who's gone through what they've gone through."

The WNBA didn't even exist when Jamila was growing up hoping to play professional ball. Women "have had to struggle for the right to play," so Jamila says it's all the more sweet when she steps on the court each night to play for the LA Sparks. "To do something I love that much and have somebody hand me a check was a little strange. It felt like I was stealing someone's money."

As the highest ranking official in the U.S. government, **MADELEINE ALBRIGHT** is arguably the most powerful woman on the globe. As the Secretary of State, it's her job to travel around the world meeting with heads of state in every country. There were no easy breaks for Madeleine—she got to where she is through hard work. She majored in political science in college, and held several related jobs in her rise to the top.

One important thing that pro Girl Bosses know is that if you want to sell something—anything—it's important to catch the eye of the customer. As marketing executives will tell you, packaging is often the key to making a sale. Companies spend millions on this issue—finding out which labels will sell their products best, from canned peas to fashion magazines. They use surveys, focus groups, and endless studies to give them an edge on the newsstand or grocery shelf. You won't go to quite those lengths, but your product's **look** will be the key to where your wares get displayed. Remember, you're also competing for space in the marketplace—you need to impress store owners so that they'll want to put your product on their shelves. And that's important in today's cyberspace world too—if your product's look is cool, Web sites will be more likely to feature them on their home page.

So How Do You Get THE LOOK?

Start with a logo. Design something on a computer or pick a stamp that you can put on your stationery, your business cards, and on your packaging. Pick something that reflects your style, and make it something eye-catching that relates to your product. For example, if you're going to sell homemade dog biscuits, you might choose a logo with a smiling dog. Look for ways to make your life easier, either by finding some computer clip art—available through a lot of simple graphics programs—or look for a rubber stamp that you can use over and over again with different colored ink.

Tag It!

Take everything you do one step further than ordinary—the point is to be as unique as possible without spending a fortune. One way to do this is through your product labels. If you're making knitted scarves, for example, create tags for them that will dangle off one end. Put the name of your business on the tag and a cute logo. If you have a Web site, put that on the tag too. That way customers who like one thing they've bought will be able to see and buy more from you. If you want customers to give you feedback through e-mail, put your e-mail address on the tag.

Of course, you don't want your tag to be so cluttered with information that it's no longer eye-catching. But short of overdoing it, get a lot of info on your tag. You can give a description, like **made of one-hundred percent merino wool,** or you could say where they're made, as in **from the back porch in Omaha,** if that's where you live. And don't forget to include any logo you've designed—you might put that on one side with other information on the back. You can punch a hole in each tag and safety-pin it to each of your products.

Packaging Your Product Like a Pro

Display It

Depending on what your business is, your display needs will be different. If you want to sell hair clips on consignment—remember that means a store agrees to carry them in exchange for a percentage of your profits—you'll have better luck if they come on a cute rack or in a specially-designed box. That's because your decorated display will add a cool look to the store. If you create your own display, the store owner won't have to worry about how to display them.

In service businesses, your needs will be different. If you're creating an online magazine or running a pet-bathing service, you won't really have a product to display. That means that your promotional materials are even more important—they'll make the only impression someone will have before hiring you.

Your Signature Style

You can incorporate a special trademark into everything you do. Using the examples from above: if you're bathing pets, you could send each one home with a red bow. Their owners will like the "dressed up" look their pets have post-bath and anyone who sees them will notice the bow. That could lead a potential customer to ask about it—and to more business down the road.

You could also incorporate your logo into your products or services. If you're designing jewelry, for example, you might decide to incorporate a tiny flower into everything you make, as a way of establishing your turf in the jewelry world and giving some designer appeal to each thing you make. Think about how many fashion empires have been built on the power of a designer signature—like the Levi trademark "button fly"or the Ralph Lauren polo player. Incorporating your logo can be powerful—make it cool so that customers will be happy to show them off!

Girl Boss Rule

Don't Be AFRAID of MISTAKES

Mistakes happen, even to the best Girl Bosses. The difference between a nitwit and a smooth Girl Boss is how those mistakes are handled. First of all—always acknowledge a blunder if it happens, whether it's yours or someone else's. But once you've done that, move on! Don't dwell on mistakes. Just fix the problem and keep moving.

If apologies are in order, make them, but don't go overboard. Don't tell the woman at the boutique where you were a week late on a delivery that you're the biggest idiot on the planet. Just figure out a way to make the best of it. For example, offer her a 5% discount and be done with it.

The same grace applies if the mistake is not yours. Don't yell and scream and make the other person feel like a moron. Remember that if the situation was reversed, you'd want to be cut some slack. So if the person you were supposed to meet with doesn't show up and you've gone across town to meet him, ask if he'll come to your neighborhood when you reschedule.

PROFILE: Sara Klinger, Katy, TX

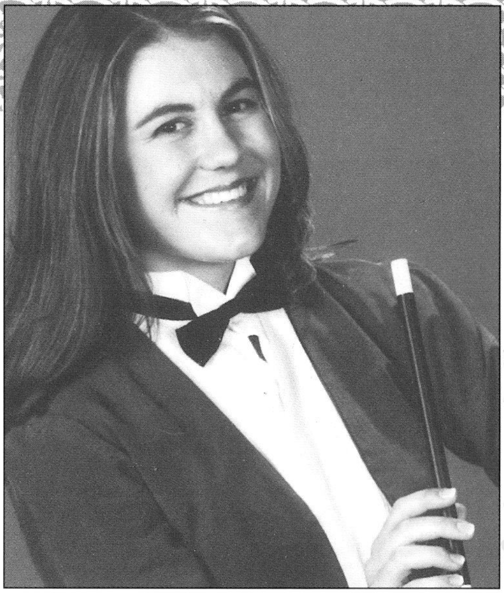

Sara Klinger got hooked on magic when she was 11 and developed her interest into a killer business that keeps her busy every weekend and most days in the summer. She started small, performing at churches and a few birthday parties, but she thought **big,** remembering to promote herself and her business by handing out business cards to everyone in the audience after each show. It worked. She started getting calls and referrals. Those word-of-mouth referrals are still the best way Sara gets new business today.

Sara says her fellow magicians help each other out, referring new customers to each other if they're already booked for a show.

Sara is constantly educating herself, learning new magic tricks, attending a magic camp each summer and developing new magic shows. She has a different show for kids and adults and has tricks she saves for close-up performances when she goes from table to table.

Sara also sets short and long-term goals. Right now her goal is to continue performing in college and to become known nationally. She's saving most of her profits to help her build a national following when she's done with school.

In her six years performing, Sara has learned to stay organized. When someone calls to hire her, she writes down all the information on note cards. She puts a card for each performance on a bulletin board above the desk in her room to remind herself of when she has a show. A few days before each show, she calls to confirm. Then after the show, she sends thank you notes and remembers to send a flier a year later to remind customers that she's ready to perform.

During the school year, Sara, who's 17 now, gives two performances each weekend and does shows almost every day in the summer. Sara charges about $80 to perform at a birthday party and has a price scale for other types of performances like corporate shows or events where she goes from table to table doing magic tricks.

Her business has taken off and Sara has socked away most of her profits, after taking a small amount out to buy clothes and other things teenagers want. Most of all, Sara performs because she loves it. "I always wanted to be in entertainment. I like knowing stuff that other people are dying to know," she says.

Fliers, business cards, and any other printed materials you might need for your biz are easy to make up on your computer. Find a local printer who is helpful and supportive and who will advise you on the basics of printed matter. Make sure you get estimates for all work and materials. Order conservatively—you can always reprint, and you may want to make revisions.

A regular piece of paper becomes a panel brochure with two folds, your message, and some artwork. A typical brochure, like Sara's is laid out with:
[outside of brochure]
(A) front cover,
(B) mail panel,
(C) intro page,
[inside of brochure]
(D) interior spread page 1,
(E) interior spread page 2, and
(F) interior spread page 3.

Like a pro Girl Boss, Sara had business cards and folding brochures printed so she'd have a way of telling people where to find her. The brochure lists the types of magic shows she puts on, along with some of the places she's performed. That gives her instant credibility—when someone wants to hire her, they know they're getting an experienced magician with a growing audience of fans.

D
2nd fold
E
1st fold
F
Specializing In
♧ Children's Magic
♡ Stand-Up Magic
♤ Strolling Magic
◇ Emcee Work
for
Birthday Parties
Banquets
Day Care Facilities
Schools
Church groups
Cocktail Parties
Scouting Events
Grand Openings
Charity Benefits
and much more!
Magician
Sara Klinger
Enjoy a Performance,
Suited to Your Occasion,
Full of Audience Participation,
Fun, Comedy,
and Mystifying Magic!
★Named best junior stage magician in Texas, 1996
★Study with internationally acclaimed magicians
★Various television appearances
★Featured on front page of "Houston Chronicle" Metropolitan Section
★Published in various journals, newsletters, newspapers
Clients Include:
Compaq Computer
Texas Children's Hospital
KinderCare
British Petroleum
Katy AARP
Strake Jesuit College Preparatory
Fluor Daniel
Second Baptist Church
Women in Magic Conference, CA
Houston Police Department
Lights in the Heights
SUEBA Corporation
B&N Construction
Yorkshire Academy
Carriage Retirement Community
and numerous day cares, schools, churches, libraries, & private parties
8½″
11″

A typical business card measures 2″×3½″ and can be horizontal or vertical, like Sara's.

Why Your Product Is Cooler Than The Rest

Being a good sales diva is more than just having great stuff to sell. It's helping a potential customer decide to buy from you instead of someone else. That can be tricky. You want to convince someone to pay hard-earned cash for something you've made, and you want them to understand its value to them. If you're selling personalized, painted socks, you want to convince someone who needs socks that your socks are better than any other socks. And even if they **don't** need socks, you want to convince them to buy a pair from you anyway. That can be a tough sell, but using the right (subtle) sales techniques, you can close the deal.

The trick is not to be too overbearing. You don't want to badger someone—especially a friend—until she's so worn down that she buys socks from you just to make you go away. That's not a great way to get a repeat customer or good word of mouth.

On the other hand, you don't want to be too easygoing. Then you'll never make the sale. If a shop owner isn't interested in your socks the first time you visit, don't be afraid to go back again a few weeks later. They'll respect your determination, and you'll begin to build a relationship—that's what good sales are all about.

Cool Sales Techniques . . .

The person you're selling to says they already have socks and besides, why are yours special?

Your answer:
I completely understand—I know there are a million kinds of socks out there. But these will be personalized and I can paint whatever you want on them. Trust me, you'll be starting a trend.

★ **Compromise—**offer a discount on the second item a person buys if they take the first one at full price. That way you sell two instead of zero.

★ **Make it clear you'll take no for an answer.** Your customer needs to know you'll put up a fair fight, but that she is ultimately in control. When she understands that she's making the decision rather than you ramming it down her throat, she'll be more likely to say yes.

★ **Sell fairly but sell completely.** Don't lie.

QUIZ—Can You Sell or What?

1 Your mom's initial reaction when you ask if you can go to a movie on a school night is ***no way.*** You:

A Pout, scream, run to your room and hope the outburst will change her mind.
B Remind her that you're completely caught up on your homework for the next day and that it's really not fair for her to make you stay home since you're old enough to decide for yourself.
C Tell her you've finished your homework for the night and make a deal: if she'll let you see the movie tonight, you'll stay home and babysit your younger brother on Friday night when she and your father want to go out. (That's the night you'd planned to have your friend come over anyway.)

2 Kids at school have been making beaded bracelets which are not difficult to make. You:

A Figure there's safety in numbers—if you make some bracelets too you're bound to sell some.
B Decide you'll never be able to compete with that much competition. You buy some yourself so at least you're not out of fashion.
C Figure bracelets are a cool gift and a hot-selling item at school. Go to a craft store, dig up some other materials, and make different bracelets to sell.

3 Your friend at school likes the bracelets you made but wants to know if she can have one for free because she's your pal. You:

A Tell her sure because she's your friend and just hope other friends don't hear about it and want freebies too.
B Tell her you'd love to, but you've got to pay for the materials you used to make the bracelets. Offer to make her a special one in whatever design she wants if she agrees to pay for one.
C Tell her you can't give them away but then feel bad and worry that she's telling your other friends how uncool you are.

4 You've decided to start a babysitting business and your aunt and uncle, who never asked you to babysit before, suddenly ask you to babysit their two kids. The catch: they don't want to pay you because you're ***family.*** You:

A Do it. How can you say no without a confrontation?
B Tell them you've started this business to make money, although you'll be happy to reserve the night for them at your normal rate.
C Refuse and tell them they're cheapskates.

Don't tell a potential customer that everything made by a competitor is awful and you're the only game in town. But don't sell yourself short either. Make sure your customer knows everything about what you have to offer and has enough information to pick yours as the best.

ANSWERS

1 C! What you're trying to do here is convince your mom to let you see the movie, not to ground you for being obnoxious. So forget answers A and B—they'll only antagonize your mom and you won't be any closer to your movie. Choose instead to be reasonable: explain to your mom what you want and balance it with a convincing reason for why you deserve it. That's the best way to be persuasive. It also helps to offer something in return.

2 C! Answers A and B will certainly get you by in life, but they won't make you a diva girl in charge. Why buy bracelets from your competition or give up on business entirely when you can turn around and capitalize on a fashion trend? Make your own original bracelets and watch your sales go through the roof.

3 B! You don't want to get in the habit of giving away your wares to friends because you could end up losing money in the end. Remember that you have to spend money on supplies. But that doesn't mean you can't cut your friends a better deal than the general public. B is the best answer: your friend will understand that you're in business but will appreciate the special deal you're giving her. The more people wear the bracelets, the more quickly they'll catch on.

4 B! Dealing with relatives can be tough—they may expect special treatment. So give it to them. Tell them they can have first dibs on weekend nights but that you'll have to charge your normal rate. That way you'll keep your business afloat and keep family ties intact.

WEB AHEAD

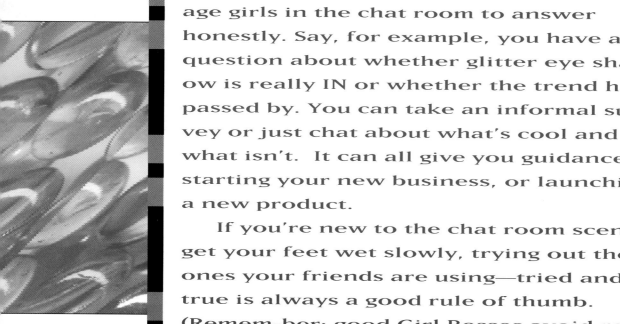

Use the WEB to Get Info for Your BIZ

Chat rooms are a great source of research and marketing. Post any questions that you have and encourage girls in the chat room to answer honestly. Say, for example, you have a question about whether glitter eye shadow is really IN or whether the trend has passed by. You can take an informal survey or just chat about what's cool and what isn't. It can all give you guidance in starting your new business, or launching a new product.

If you're new to the chat room scene, get your feet wet slowly, trying out the ones your friends are using—tried and true is always a good rule of thumb. (Remem-ber: good Girl Bosses avoid re-inventing the wheel.) Make sure you like the tone of the conversations you see posted and get a feel for whether you're in a place with girls like yourself. Once you've found the chat room that's right for you, let loose—use the girls on the other end of the modem to talk about what ever's on your mind.

How to Get Business

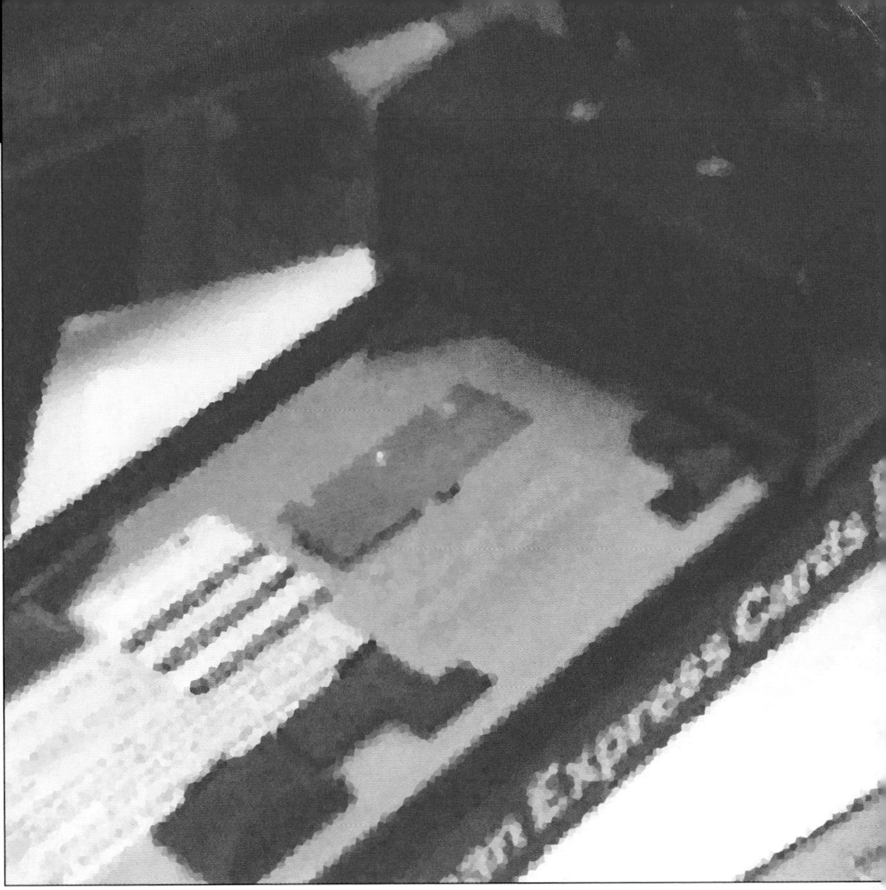

Wherever you go, there will be people who need your services or products, whether you're offering plant-watering services or making keychains. The trick is getting them to hire you. It can be a delicate balance—you don't want to seem too pushy (read: desperate), but you don't want to be spineless either.

That's why publicity materials are so important. They give people an idea of what you can do for them, as well as a way of reaching you later. That way they don't feel pressured to hire you on the spot, but they do know where to find you when their plants need watering or when they need a new keychain.

Pass out your fliers or business cards in places that are related to your business. For example, if you're making workout duffel bags with special pockets for shampoo and things, hand out business cards at the local gym—you could even take samples. Or if your potential customers are less targeted, go to parks, coffee houses, or your lunchroom at school. (Just remember that if you're going to hand out fliers outside a store, school, or business, you'll need permission from the owner or principal.)

Don't be shy about accepting business from your friends or family! If your relatives want to be your first customers, there's no reason why you shouldn't let them. They'll have the pleasure of knowing they helped you get started, and you'll have the first sales you need to grow. They'll probably brag to friends and even more business will come your way. You'll also have the benefit of trying out your first few plant feedings or keychain experiments on people you know. That way if there's a big disaster, you know your family will still be right behind you, helping you figure out how to do things differently next time.

Online Magazine Resources

You can get a lot more from the Web than just great information. Look for articles written by and for Girl Bosses—you'll find them at many of the magazine sites. When you're working at home and feeling a bit disconnected from the rest of the world, it can really help to connect with the "voices" of other teens, whether they're Girl Bosses or not. The same goes for chat rooms you like. Use them to stay on top of trends, make new contacts, and reconnect with the outside world.

Check these out:

✦ **Blue Jean Magazine at** http://www.bluejeanmag.com

✦ **Cybergrrl at** http://www.cybergrrl.com

✦ **Girl Power at** http://www.girlpower.com

✦ **New Moon at** http://www.newmoon.org

✦ **Teen Voices Online at** http://www.teenvoices.com

SECTION 5

Dollar Smart

How Much to Invest in Your Biz

In order to buy supplies and get your business started, you generally have to invest SOMETHING. But how do you know how much to sink into your start-up? First of all, the amount you'll need to get things rolling will depend on the kind of business you want to have. If it's going to be a pet-bathing service, for example, you'll have to invest in washing tubs, soaps, some brushes, and towels. You'll also have to spend some money to advertise your services. On the other hand, if you're going to build a business around tutoring, your costs may all be advertising-related.

So here's your start for putting together your start-up budget. Write down all of the supplies you'll need to run your business. Supplement your brainstorming with research—ask other people with similar businesses, surf the Internet, and read any relevant articles you can get your hands on. Your research should also include visiting the stores where you'll get supplies—figure out where you can get the best deal, and how much your basic supplies will cost.

Publicity

The other important investment you'll make is in publicity. It's the key to drumming up business and to the success of your start-up. You don't need to spend a small fortune on professionally printed advertisements, or buy time on a local T.V. channel to launch a successful publicity campaign. You can do a lot of your work at home if your family has a computer. (See the **Getting the Word Out** section on promotional ideas.)

Develop your promotional plan—factoring in ideas like business cards, stationery, and fliers—and estimate what they'll cost. Be sure to add them to your budgeted start-up costs for the business. And remember, once you start making sales, you'll have more money to invest later (after you've paid back any loans and replaced your savings.) Once you're really up and running, you can expand your P.R. campaign even more.

Materials

Depending on what kind of business you have, your materials may cost a lot or practically nothing. Here's where it's especially important to shop around so you know you're getting the best prices. Don't be afraid to ask for a bargain. Store owners will sometimes negotiate on the price of materials if you're buying large amounts—that's called a bulk discount.

But be careful not to go overboard when buying supplies. Don't buy enough to make 200 beaded headbands, for example. Because if they don't sell well and you decide to make beaded necklaces instead,

you'll be stuck with all those unused headbands. Once you see how much you're selling, you can decide how much more to invest in materials. Or maybe you'll decide to concentrate on promoting your business and spend more money on that for a while.

Try to avoid laying out huge sums of cash yourself. If you plan to paint on the backs of jean jackets, for example, ask customers to buy a jean jacket themselves and bring it to you to paint. Once you've made some money you'll be able to buy the jackets yourself (perhaps at a bulk discount), and sell them already painted.

Here's a chart to help you figure out how much you've spent on each category of start-up expenses. There's a column for your **budgeted** expenses and a separate column for your **actual** expenses. That way, if you get an unexpected discount on your photocopying costs, you may have more to spend somewhere else. There's always something that costs more than you think it will and something you'll be able to get on sale!

✓ **Materials You Bought**

✓ **Estimated Cost**

✓ **Actual Cost**

Materials You Bought	Estimated Cost	Actual Cost

Raising the Cash You Need

Financing a new business can be tough, especially when you're doing it for the first time. Don't expect banks to line up to loan you millions of dollars.

Generally, to get a loan, you have to prove that you have some type of collateral—something of value that you own, like a home, a car, or an existing business—that will secure your loan. In other words, banks want to know that if you don't pay them back, they have a chance of getting their money back by taking your collateral. Early in your Girl Boss career, you're not likely to have much to your name, so banks won't want to take a big risk on your venture.

But that doesn't mean that you're out of luck. You can save the money you need to start up a new business, either by working for a while in a job that's related to what you want to do—this gives you the benefit of learning while making some money—or you can just find the best job you can that helps you build up a stash of dough.

Also, if your parents are willing, you could arrange a system where they loan you some start-up funds in exchange for a percentage of your profits. But if you choose this route, think of your parents like a financial institution: you don't want to ruin your future credit by failing to repay your parents what they loaned you. Work out a payment plan and stick to it—Girl Bosses don't default!

And get creative! If you can't afford to pay someone for a service you need, barter. For example, if you need to find someone to pass out fliers advertising the concert your band is giving, offer to wash your friend's car or help her babysit one night if she'll help you out. You don't have to pay for everything with cash.

RESOURCES TO CHECK

- The Directory of Directories (at the local library)
- The Encyclopedia of Associations (at the local library)
- The Internet—through search engines like
  www.yahoo.com
  www.snap.com
  www.inktomi.com, and
  www.altavista.com—

Put in key words like **association** and the type of group you're looking for.

Jennifer Kushell

President of the Young Entrepreneurs Network

When Jennifer Kushell was a teenager in Encino, California, she already knew she had what it took to be a Girl Boss. She was serious about going into business for herself and kept pursuing her dreams until she had established a video production company that offered its services to college tours and created a safety seminar for young women.

She founded the Young Entrepreneurs Network because there was no place for young people who were starting businesses to go for information and networking. So she filled the void herself.

Just what a Girl Boss should do!

When you set out to get informed, think of it as a fact-finding mission. Plan on collecting as much as you can and putting the information into one organized place, like a set of folders or a three-ring binder. That way, you can flip through your resources when you need them and won't waste valuable time searching through piles to find them. Get excited about being thorough. Think of it as a challenge to scrape up every great piece of information related to the business you want to run.

Arrange your research into a couple of categories. Look for examples of Girl Bosses who are doing the kind of work you want to do. Or even dig up a few who are doing different things but whose style you like. For example, if you want to create a zine, search at the library for stories about girls who have started zines. Look for stories on Girl Bosses who have started up other kinds of publications, or businesses that have a similar focus. Keep a file of their stories.

Then look for any instructional materials about how to create zines. Look for Web sites that deal with the zine scene and collect everything you can find in a different folder or section of your binder.

Also keep your eyes open for any televised documentaries or other programs—especially news magazine shows—that will fuel your research. Take notes and keep them together. Your notes can also include any interviews or ideas gathered from conversations with mentors or Girl Bosses you meet.

Once you've collected all your information, you won't be starting from scratch. You'll have the benefit of specific do's and don'ts that relate to your business ideas. Your collection of information should be personalized and specific to your biz, so tailor it to focus on whatever areas you need to investigate the most.

Of course, at some point, once you've done your reading, your interviewing, and your research, you'll be ready to get going. You'll have figured out how to bankroll your first few steps and learned what you need to get started. This is the point when you need to take your ideas and try them out on the marketplace. Then your learning will come from experience—and you'll be on your way to being a professional.

Money cannot buy happiness, but can certainly hire it for short periods in expensive restaurants or careless weeks on Austrian skis.

—Irma Kurtz, writer

LADY BOSS Role Models from T.V.

Barbara Stanwyck

As ranch-owner Victoria Barkley, on *The Big Valley*

Dixie Carter

As design firm-owner Julia Sugarbaker, on *Designing Women*

Candice Bergen

As hard-nosed news anchor Murphy Brown

Mary Tyler Moore

As Mary Richards, one of the first independent working women on T.V., on *The Mary Tyler Moore Show*

Behind every successful man is a surprised woman.

—MARYON PEARSON

Barbara Stanwyck in *The Big Valley*

Chart Your Progress

One great thing you can do to stay organized and remind yourself of how much ground you've covered is to chart your progress—literally. That means making a chart that shows your goals and allows you to mark them off as you go.

Make something really graphic that charges you up each time you look at it. You might decide to list your goals on a large chart in ascending order. Then connect the dots and see the mountain you've climbed

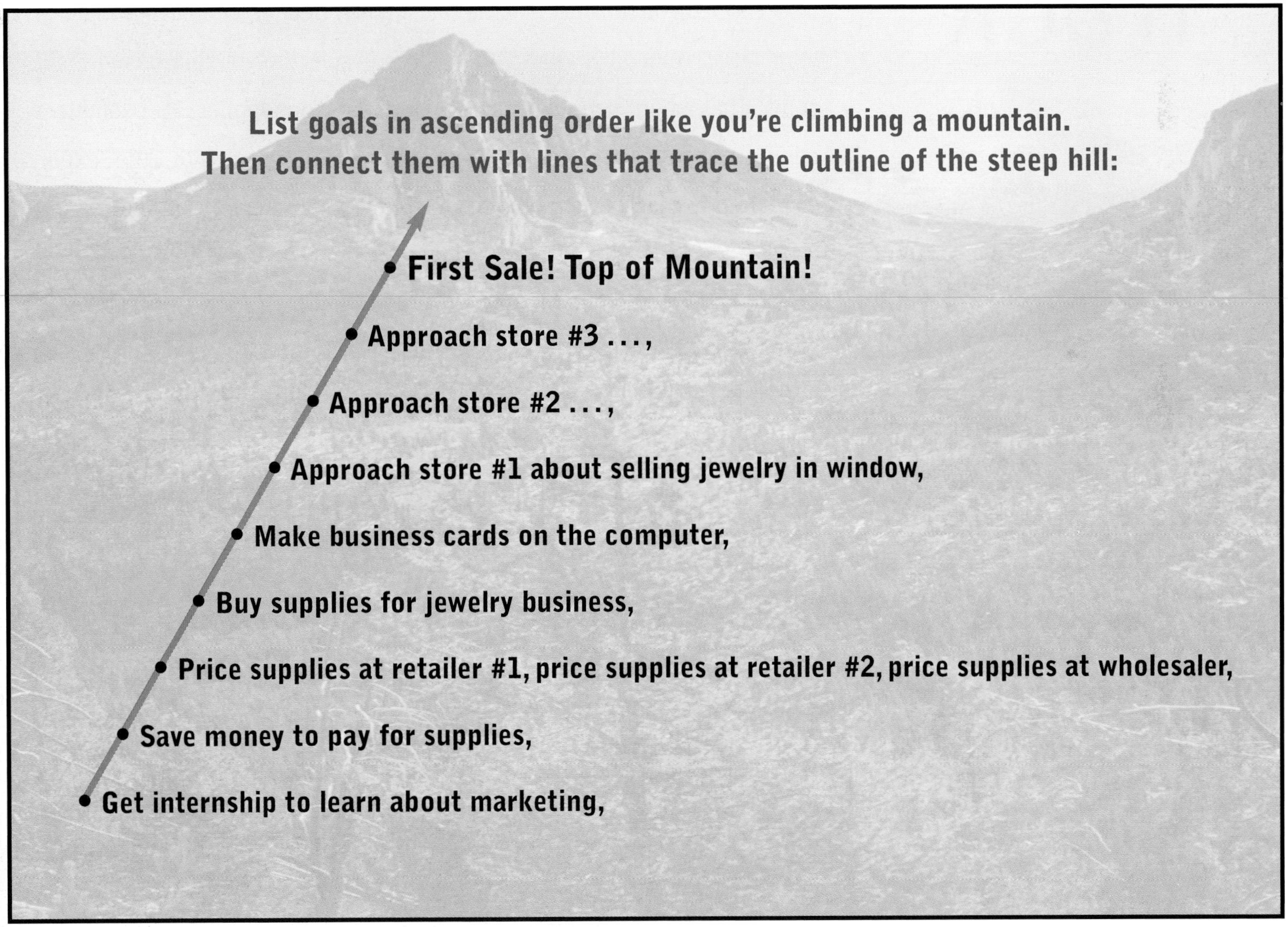

List goals in ascending order like you're climbing a mountain.
Then connect them with lines that trace the outline of the steep hill:
First Sale! Top of Mountain!
Approach store #3 . . . ,
Approach store #2 . . . ,
Approach store #1 about selling jewelry in window,
Make business cards on the computer,
Buy supplies for jewelry business,
Price supplies at retailer #1, price supplies at retailer #2, price supplies at wholesaler,
Save money to pay for supplies,
Get internship to learn about marketing,

Keeping Track of Your Cash

If all goes according to plan, your business will be generating profits. Of course that probably won't happen right away, so don't get stressed if you're working hard and still not rolling in the big bucks—most businesses start slowly and build until they turn a profit. So **stick with it.**

Once you do start making sales, you'll need to keep a few things in mind. First, remember what you've already spent to get your business going. That means keeping track of your costs for supplies, for example—and also any other expenses you've had for photocopying or other expenses related to marketing. You have to subtract these expenses before you can start racking up profits.

Second, you need to have a way of keeping track of what you've spent and what you've made. (See the worksheet on the following pages.) And third, you'll need to decide what to do with all your profits! Will you save them? Will you spend them on more supplies to keep the business going? Will you use them to splurge on treats for yourself and your friends? Or a combination?

Don't Do This—Mistakes and Traps to Avoid. *Everyone has at least one thing they can think of that they wish they'd done differently. You'll look back some day and have your own share of experiences that will make you cringe. But you can learn a lot from the fearless females that have gone before you, and maybe even avoid some of the bigger drags.*

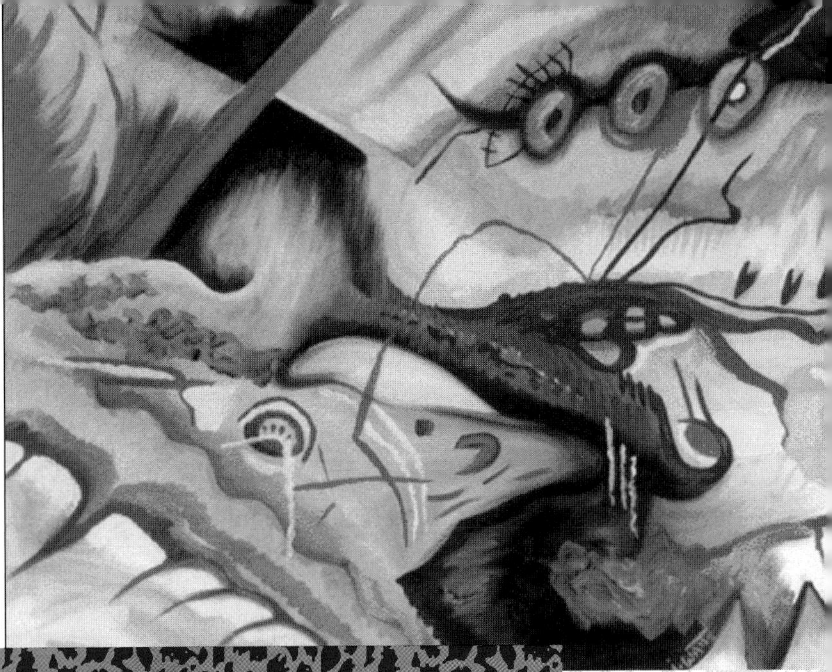

Mistakes

✪ Shayna wanted a job so badly she offered to do the first assignment for free. She did the first assignment and never got called again. The company made off like a bandit.

✪ Lucy forgot to sign a contract with the company that hired her to draw cartoons. She drew her first batch of ten, according to the assignment she was given. The company wanted to see ten more, saying they didn't like the first ones enough to use them. Looking back, she wished she'd negotiated a "kill fee," which meant that she'd get paid for the work she did even if the company opted not to use them. Otherwise, she could keep drawing, ten at a time, forever.

✪ Karen told a non-profit documentary filmmaker that she'd only do calligraphy on invitations to his film premiere if he paid her "the normal rate," which was more than they usually paid. She ended up not getting the assignment and wishing she'd agreed to do it for less, as a partial donation to the project. She also could have done them for free and arranged to put her logo on the invitations for potential future business.

✪ Jana was making t-shirts, and didn't want to turn away business from a clothing store because she was just starting out—she didn't think she could afford to be picky. But she had a bad feeling about the store owner from the beginning. The owner couldn't decide on which dyed shirts she wanted and asked Jana to make several types to show her before she'd agree to carry them in her store. She ended up being so picky Jana had to redye her t-shirts multiple times. The lesson cost her a fortune.

Lessons Learned

✗ **Put everything in writing.**
You'll always have something to refer to if someone's trying to take advantage of you.

✗ **Always be flexible.**
There are no hard and fast rules and you can sometimes trade profits for publicity.

✗ **Don't be too desperate.**
Feel free to turn away some business that isn't worth it.

Money Worksheet

Once you've got money rolling in, your first instinct may be to put it in the bank or into your wallet and forget about it. Big mistake. Part of the fun of having a business and making extra money is knowing how much you've made. And unless you have a photographic memory, the easiest way to keep track of everything is to fill in a handy chart like the one on this page.

Our sample chart is based on a hypothetical jewelry business. The Girl Boss who's selling the jewelry line spent $20 to photocopy fliers, which list all her products and show pictures of them. The cost is divided among her five product lines. The expense column ($ Invested) shows the amount she spent to buy supplies for each type of jewelry. The next two columns show the number of each type of bracelet, necklace, or earrings she made and the number she sold of each.

The last column shows the amount of money she was paid for each piece of jewelry. The calculations show how to figure out how much you've made, how much you've spent and how much your overall profits are. Just plug in the numbers from the charts below.

Number sold
x Price Per Piece
Total Revenues

Total Revenues
- Total $ Invested
Total Profits

Product Line	$ Invested	Number Made	Number Sold	Selling Price Per Piece
Beaded Wire Bracelet	$9 on wire $15 on beads plus $4 to photocopy fliers	20	15	$6
Double-Wrap Wire Bracelet	$13 on wire, $4 for fliers	15	12	$5
String-Beaded Bracelet	$4 for string $20 for beads $4 for fliers	15	10	$5
Beaded Necklace	$10 on wire $25 on beads $4 for fliers	10	6	$10
Twisted Wire Earrings	$6 for cardboard mounting, $10 for wire $4 for fliers	20	14	$8

Here's how to calculate the profits on our Girl Boss' bracelet sales:

Beaded Wire Bracelet:

15 sold
x $6. Per Piece
$90. Total Revenues
– $28. Invested
$62. Profit

Double-Wrap Wire Bracelet:

12 sold
x $5. Per Piece
$60. Total Revenues
– $17. Invested
$43. Profit

String-Beaded Bracelet:

10 sold
x $5. Per Piece
$50. Total Revenues
– $28. Invested
$22. Profit

Twisted-Wire Earrings:

14 sold
x $8. Per Piece
$112. Total Revenues
– $20. Invested
$92. Profit

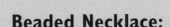

Beaded Necklace:

6 sold
x $10. Per Piece
$60. Total Revenues
– $39. Invested
$21. Profit

QUIZ—Do You Have Dollars Sense?

It's not easy to manage money. Companies hire teams of experts to do it right, so don't worry if it's not obvious to you in the beginning. You don't have to be a genius with spreadsheets (you don't even have to know what they are) to run your business. Just try to use your common sense, stay organized, and keep your eye on your business goals.

You're collecting money from a store that purchased 20 of your hand-stenciled boxes. They owe you $300 and they insist on paying you in cash. You:

1. Make sure they give you an itemized, signed receipt that shows how many boxes they bought and how much they paid you for each one. Then you put the money straight in the bank.
2. Suspect that they're doing something underhanded like paying you under the table so they can avoid paying taxes or something, and refuse to do business with them again.
3. Insist on a company check, then cash it, run to the mall and spend all the money on a couple of new outfits.

Your profits are starting to add up and a friend asks if she can borrow a big chunk of it to get her car back from the tow yard so her parents don't find out. You:

1. Offer to drive her there and use your best negotiating skills to get the tow charge reduced, but insist that she come up with the money herself.
2. Give her the money and pray she pays you back.
3. Tell her that you're offended that she'd ask to borrow money.

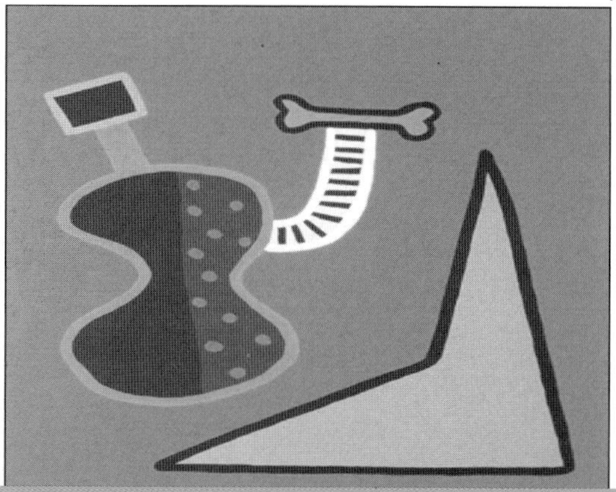

Your business is profitable! Now you have to decide what to do with the money—you want to save for a car and don't want to tempt yourself now. You:

1. Open a certificate of deposit (CD) account at your bank because you'll be able to get a higher interest rate on the money you've earned if you agree to leave it in the bank for a year or more.
2. Keep the money in a box under your bed because you never know when you'll need a few bucks.
3. Invest in risky stocks, hoping your money will grow into a huge pile of dough by the time you hit college.

ANSWERS: Go for number one.

Jane Wyman, as *Lucy Gallant* in the 1955 movie—one of the first lady bosses of the big screen.

In politics, if you want anything said, ask a man; if you want anything done, ask a woman.

—MARGARET THATCHER

Money Worries and Ways to Beat Them

WORRY: ***If I spend money on supplies and brochures and my business doesn't succeed, I'll have less money than when I started.***

REALITY: Spend wisely and consider the investment you make an education in how the business world works. You're getting your education the best way possible.

WORRY: ***If my business does well and I make money, my parents will think I don't need an allowance any more and I'll be working harder for the same amount of money.***

REALITY: That's easy—ask your parents to put the money they would have paid you as allowance into a special bank account for college.

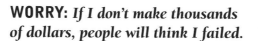

WORRY: ***If I don't make thousands of dollars, people will think I failed.***

REALITY: People will think you started a business and consider you a great success because of it. Remember: It's no one's business how much money you make.

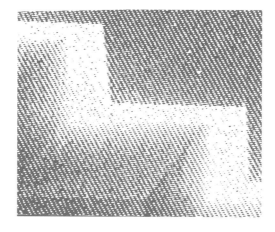

WORRY: ***I'm not too organized and I'll lose track of how much I've spent and how much I've made.***

REALITY: Keeping track isn't that tough. Set up a simple notebook with one page for expenses, one for money you've received, and one to keep track of the amount you plan to save. You'll get the hang of it once you see the potential profits you can make.

WORRY: ***If I make a lot of money and people like me, I won't know who my real friends are.***

REALITY: Once again, your profits are no one's business but your own. If you suspect that you have new friends because they think you're loaded, tell them you're not making much money and see if they go away. They probably won't.

WORRY: ***I don't have enough money to start my business.***

REALITY: You can start your business by getting a part-time job and committing the money you earn to your business fund. The job can be the first step in your business plan.

GOOD DOLLAR TIPS

- ❊ **Shop around before you buy anything.**
- ❊ **Look for discounts by buying in bulk.**
- ❊ **Look for jobs that you can do cheap on your home PC.**
- ❊ **Recycle!**
- ❊ **Have plants in your office—it's a cheap way to upgrade your surroundings.**
- ❊ **Write down everything related to your finances.**

Camp $tart-Up

If you're a Girl Boss wannabe, aged 13 to 18, Camp $tart-Up could be the place for you. It's a summer program that allows you to work with a team on a business idea—from start to finish. The camp takes you through the steps you'll need to run your business, including researching your ideas, creating marketing materials, and negotiating for what you need. You'll be supervised by a team of pros and business women who teach from experience.

Check out camp $tart-up at the web site for Independent Means at HTTP://WWW.ANINCOMEOFHEROWN.COM

While you're at their web site, you can also enter a competition to help finance your business dream. The National Business Plan Competition, run by Independent Means, allows you to describe your business idea, as well as your plans for making it a reality. You may win a cash award, but even more valuable is the experience of outlining your goals and organizing them into a real business plan. You'll realize where the holes are—what information is missing and what you still have to learn. But best of all you'll be able to describe exactly what you want to do and how you plan to tackle it. Then nothing will be able to stop you.

Great Financial Books Written by Women

- ***The Black Woman's Guide to Financial Independence: Smart Ways to Take Charge of Your Money, Build Wealth, and Achieve Financial Security***
  —Cheryl Broussard

- ***Every Woman's Guide to Investing: 11 Steps to Financial Independence and Security***
  —Francie Prince and Douglas Pi

- ***The Enterprising Woman***
  —Mari Florence

- ***The Financially Confident Woman***
  —Mary Hunt

- ***Finding Your Financial Freedom: Every Woman's Guide to Success***
  —Joyce Ward

- ***Grants at a Glance: A Directory of Financial Resources for Women in Science***

- ***When Are You Entitled to New Underwear and Other Major Financial Decisions: Making Your Money Dreams Come True***
  —Eileen Michaels

- ***Big Book of Opportunities for Women***
  —Elizabeth A. Olson

- ***Dollars for College: The Quick Guide to Financial Aid for Women in All Fields (Dollars for College Series)***
  —Elizabeth A. Olson

- ***The Higher Education Moneybook for Women & Minorities, 1997: A Directory of Scholarships, Fellowships, Internships, Grants & Loans*** *(1997 Ed.)*
  —Doris Marie Bruce-Young

SECTION 6

Advice from Girl Bosses

Finding Good Mentors and Other Help

Good Mentors, Friends, and Helpful Chat Rooms

One of the best things any Girl Boss can do is find a great mentor. All this really means is finding someone who can be your role model. While you're at it, find **two** mentors: one who you can really get to know and approach for help, and another who is a public figure you'd like to use as a role model from afar.

MENTOR NUMBER ONE

Choose a mentor who has the qualities you crave. Think about some of the great lady bosses of all time: Madame C. J. Walker, Lucille Ball, and Katharine Graham. Check for information about them on the Internet, scrounge up books from the library, ask your mom and dad what they know about them. Bottom line, you should get the real dirt, stories about what kind of bosses they were (or are) and stories about how they reached their goals.

Kate Mulgrew, as Captain Janeway—Sci-fi Boss on *Star Trek: Voyager*

MENTOR NUMBER TWO

For your other mentor—the one you'll actually meet and hopefully work with over time—you also should do your research carefully. She may be a teacher whose style you admire, a relative who has a cool career, or a family friend who owns a business. She could even be a **friend** of a family friend—spread your network wide. Ask your parents and their friends if they know someone you can approach.

The most important thing when seeking a mentor is to know what you want her to do for you. Obviously you don't want it to be a lot of work for her. But remember that people like to help—you may think that the young executive at your mom's firm can't possibly remember what it was like to be your age, but think again. It wasn't that long ago that she was in your shoes.

And remember that your mentor doesn't have to be a hard-nosed dragon lady who runs a 200-person company. Some lady bosses will have six kids, while others will be single parents. Some great lady bosses will run their own big departments, while others will be freelance journalists who work from home. Each lady boss you meet can offer you something different—don't be afraid to talk to a few people until you find the right fit. Your mentor should feel more like an older sister than a parent.

Once you've found someone you look up to, make sure you can talk to her too. You need to feel comfortable sharing your ideas, fears and questions without worrying that you're wasting her valuable time or saying something stupid. No one expects you to know everything. If you did, you wouldn't need a mentor.

Once your mentor has taken an interest in you and your future, she won't want to see you spinning your wheels doing things that won't work out. She'll help guide you in the right direction because once she's invested her time, she'll want a good return on her investment. **That's you.** She'll want to see how things turn out, so don't forget to keep her in the loop, no matter how successful your business becomes.

Astronaut **Eileen M. Collins** occupies the commander's station on the Space Shuttle Atlantis' flight deck during rendezvous operations with Russia's Mir Space Station.

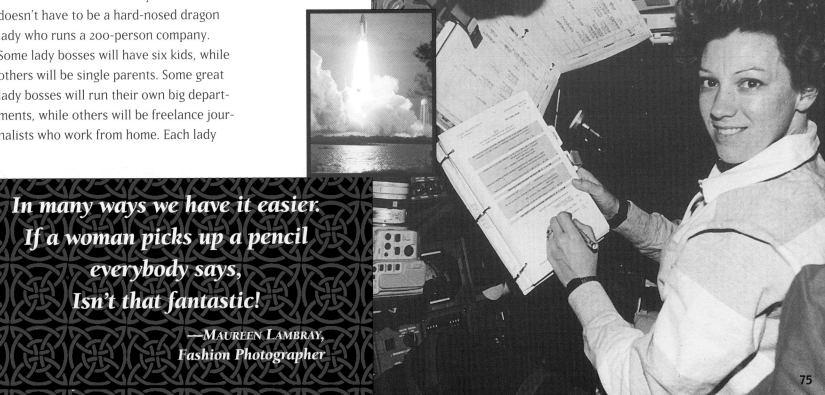

In many ways we have it easier. If a woman picks up a pencil everybody says, Isn't that fantastic!

—Maureen Lambray, Fashion Photographer

Qualities to Look for in a Mentor

- ✣ **Positive attitude.** If she could do it, so can you.
- ✣ **A great work life and some kind of a personal life.** You don't want to get advice from someone who grinds herself into the ground for the sake of her career at the cost of all else.
- ✣ **Ambition.** You want to see how she laid out her goals and went after them, so you can figure out how to do the same.
- ✣ **Enthusiasm.** She should be excited about what she does and excited about what you will one day do.
- ✣ **Success.** She doesn't have to be running the world, but her Girl Boss instincts have to be working for her to be a good role model.
- ✣ **Willingness.** Even the best-sounding role model has to be willing to take you under her wing. You can't force it. Wait until you find the right match.

Signs You've Got the Wrong Mentor

- ✣ She tells you the way to get ahead is to wear a short skirt and a tight top and to develop a gay little laugh.
- ✣ You call her office to set an appointment, and her assistant calls you back and says she won't be available for six months, but she'll pencil you in at that time if you want.
- ✣ She shows you around her office, pointing out her toothbrush, shower, and sleeping compartment because she almost never gets a chance to go home.
- ✣ She tells you you'll never be able to . . .
- ✣ She says it's too late to start all the really great businesses because the good ideas are taken, but you can always get a second-rate job.
- ✣ She talks down to you and frequently uses words like stupid, lame, and impossible.

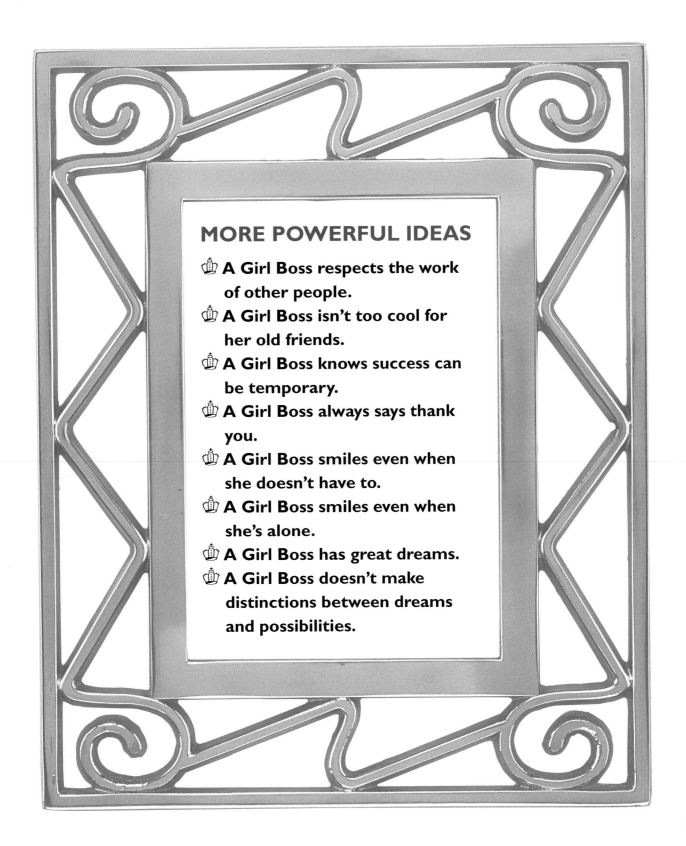

MORE POWERFUL IDEAS

- A Girl Boss respects the work of other people.
- A Girl Boss isn't too cool for her old friends.
- A Girl Boss knows success can be temporary.
- A Girl Boss always says thank you.
- A Girl Boss smiles even when she doesn't have to.
- A Girl Boss smiles even when she's alone.
- A Girl Boss has great dreams.
- A Girl Boss doesn't make distinctions between dreams and possibilities.

What Makes Professionals Look That Way

Being a professional is really in the eye of the beholder—in other words, if you look and act the part, no one will doubt that you're a goddess boss ready to take the world by storm. That means silly-sounding things like greeting everyone you meet with a solid handshake. It also means dressing like you want to be taken seriously. Your appearance sends a message about how you perceive yourself and how you want others to perceive you. But that doesn't mean you have to look like a bombshell to earn your way to a solid business.

A professional appearance is simple—it means taking pride in your appearance. That means **not** arriving at a business meeting with dark circles under your eyes and a rat's nest for a hairdo. It does mean taking a shower, putting on something that communicates your individual style and smiling when you walk in the door.

Be an Advocate.

Professional Girl Bosses know how to share their ideas and enthusiasm with other Girl Bosses. This kind of networking is critical to any new business—don't be shy about making contacts with other girls and women in similar fields. You'll be amazed at the different ways you'll find to work together, save on costs, or combine forces to increase your total impact.

Be Open!

If you worry too much about people taking your ideas, you'll miss out on your best networking chances. Real Girl Bosses know that encouraging others is the best thing you can do for yourself. There's no reason you can't have friendly relationships with all of your fellow Girl Bosses—even your competitors. You could end up with a customer, a business confidante, a friend, or even a partner. Seek out organizations of women business owners in your area, tap into their Web sites, get on their mailing lists, and do what you can to support them. You never know when you'll want them to support **you**.

TRUE FACTS

- The number of people employed by women-owned businesses has increased about **180%** over the past decade to 326,000 employees
- Women provide jobs for **one out of every four** employees at American companies
- States with the most women-owned businesses: California, New York, Illinois, Texas, and Michigan

Source: *Working Woman* magazine

Dreams are necessary to life.

—Anaïs Nin, *The Diary of Anaïs Nin*

List Your Objectives: The Business Plan

The first thing you should do when you start a business is write a simple business plan. Your business plan doesn't have to be a hundred pages long, but it **is** really important in defining your purpose. It will force you to do your research, and write down all of your objectives—basically your goals for growing the business into a full-fledged venture. The purpose of creating a business plan is to give you a point of reference later as the business starts to grow. You'll be able to look back and make sure you're sticking to your goals and seeing them through.

This all sounds obvious, but you'd be surprised how easy it is to get sidetracked. For example, you may decide you've always dreamed of starting a poetry journal—so you recruit the best poets you can find and compile their material. You go to newsstands to get them to carry the journals on their racks and the first few tell you that humor magazines sell better. You want your venture to take off so you figure you'll write a few humor magazines and then switch to poetry once you've built a name. What if the humor magazines start selling? Before you know it you're several years into it and still no poetry journal.

Here's where your business plan just might remind you to put your foot down and get back to your original objective. On the other hand, you may reread your business plan and decide to put it on hold for awhile. Either way, it's good to have your initial objective for reference. Don't give up on your dreams, no matter what anyone tells you. The best business plans are based on them.

Even the most successful Girl Bosses occasionally have to reevaluate and make sure things are running according to plan. Sometimes you need to shift directions or grab the reins.

Gloria Steinem is one Girl Boss who kept an eye on a project she started, even though it has been more than 25 years since that day. Gloria Steinem, founder of *Ms.* Magazine, joined a group of investors to buy the bi-monthly magazine from its most recent owners, MacDonald Communications. Under its new great lady bosses, the magazine continues to hold onto its feminist edge and to serve as a place for contemporary voices of women to be heard. The magazine carries no ads and depends mainly on newsstand and subscription sales for its revenues.

GIRL BOSS ADVICE: Learn to Listen

Knowing When to Sit Back and Take It All In

You can learn a lot by keeping quiet and hearing what's going on around you. It sounds like common sense, but you'd be surprised at how few people know how to do it well. Some of the best business ideas will come from just listening to what people around you are saying.

You'll realize that mastering the art of listening is easier said than done. It's sometimes tempting to be one of the voices in the group conversation or to feel obligated to say something. We all know what it's like: instead of being a good listener, you find yourself frantically trying to think of something to say. But instead, try taking a breather from the conversation for 15 minutes and just **listen** to what everyone else is saying.

That's when you'll hear your friend say there are no good lip gloss flavors. Instead of jumping in and agreeing, be an observer. Sit back and listen to whether your other friends agree. Take each comment from your friends and family as a mini-piece of research about the consumer market. Each time you hear someone complain about something, try to figure out a solution. That solution could be your business.

You can also get plenty of information from people you don't know. If you're sitting in a coffeehouse or standing in line at the movies, listen to the idle conversation around you for first-hand reviews of anything and everything. You'll hear what people think of the hottest movie stars, the newest trends, the dishiest gossip. All for free.

Listen for Feedback

Listening can also be useful once your business is up and running. Ask for opinions and really listen to what people say about your business ideas. For example, if you ask ten friends what they think about your plan to make furry toilet seat covers, you'll get a variety of opinions. Some friends may laugh in your face. Others may be supportive no matter what. But tell your friends what you want and you'll be much more likely to get it—tell them you want them to be completely honest, or ask them if they'd buy one and if so, what colors they'd buy. And if you get the sense that people are ambivalent, ask more people. Don't read something into someone's response that isn't there. At the same time, make sure you're getting the real dirt.

When possible, be sure to ask people who are representative of your target market. In other words, if you're planning to sell fake fur collars as a hip fashion statement, ask for opinions from people who you think would buy them. Don't ask Aunt Harriet what she thinks if you know for a fact she'll say they're the craziest thing she's ever heard of.

Listen to What's News

The big issues in the news can be great business inspirations. That doesn't mean you should make joke t-shirts about the latest politician in trouble. It means listening to real information that's bound to shape trends. If you hear that the president is beginning an eight-year campaign to improve the educational system, think about businesses that relate to it. Your business will be much easier to publicize if you can tie it in to a national trend or a big issue.

Take Advice

Be open to all and every piece of advice. That means that you listen to everything, but only act on some of it. Remember that all advice should be taken with a grain of salt, keeping in mind the motivations and the smarts of the person doling it out. Some advice could turn out to be invaluable, and some should be left just where you found it. But accept anyone's advice gladly (it can't hurt) and decide later on whether it makes any sense for your business.

But that's just a little helpful advice . . .

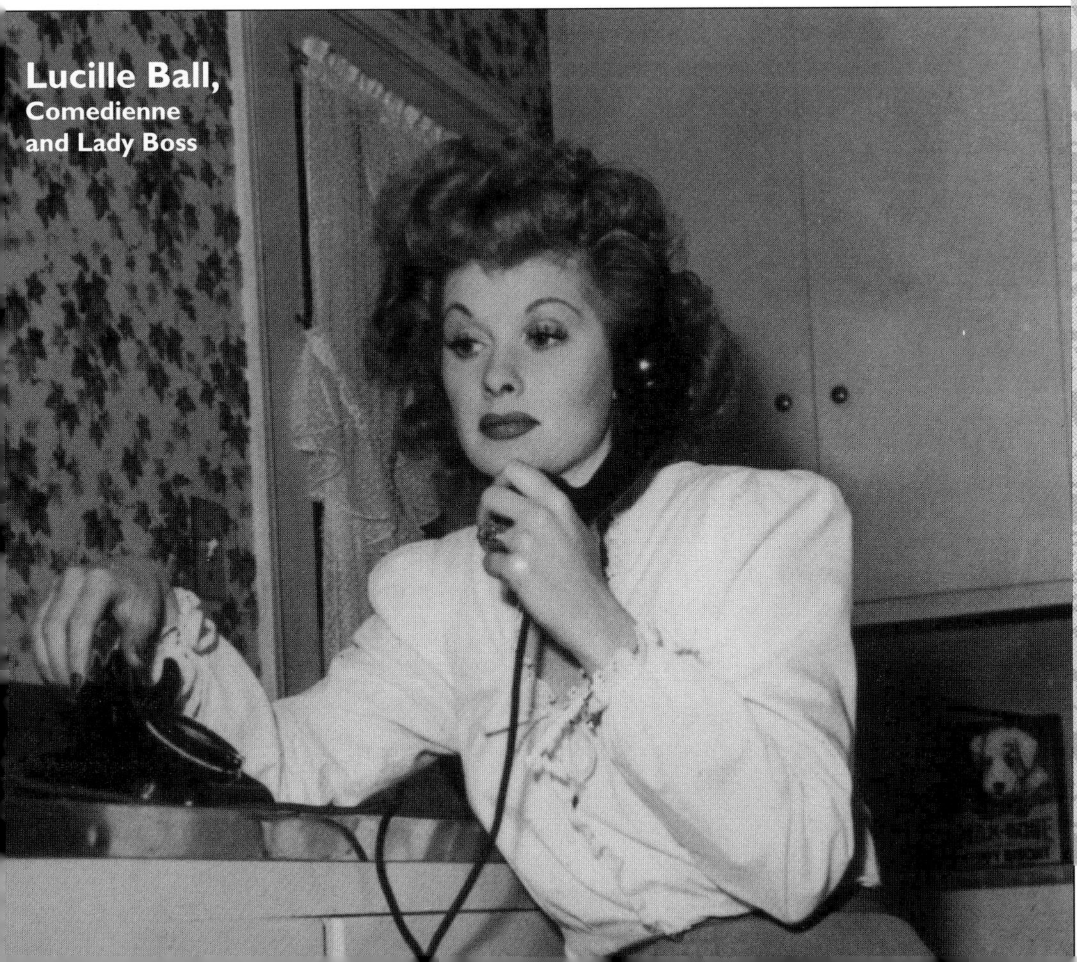

Lucille Ball,
Comedienne and Lady Boss

WOMEN BUSINESS OWNERS HAVE POWER . . .

. . . and companies are sitting up and listening

The U.S. Department of Labor predicts that by the year 2000, about half of the businesses in America will be owned by women.

Corporate America has taken note. Banks have special loan programs for women business owners, and advertisers have begun targeting women specifically, rather than relying on the age-old myth that businesses are better run by men.

Take a look at some of the biggest recent advertising campaigns:

- **Mountain Dew, for example is using cool snowboarding girls in their ads, saluting the culture of athletic women who rule.**
- **Nike is another company that launched a series of ads featuring Girl Boss athletes like Sheryl Swoopes and Dawn Staley, paying tribute to the real movers and shakers on the sports scene.**

Some companies—including the big long distance telephone giants, banks, and technology manufacturers—have started programs geared specifically to women. They're smart. They know they need to get hip to the booming trend of women in business if they're going to sell their services to the businesses of the future.

That's girl power!

To love what you do and feel that it matters—how could anything be more fun?

—Katharine Graham, *Chairperson*, **Washington Post**

The Power of 3

There's something magic about the number three. Public speakers are told to repeat a point 3 times if they really want the audience to remember it. The idea is that if someone hears a point **once,** they may notice that it's interesting, but then move on to your next comment. If you say it **twice,** they notice that you said something really great, but won't be able to remember it later. But if you repeat it a **third** time, it will be firmly impressed upon their memory.

You've made your point!

The Power of the Pen

Never underestimate the power of putting things in writing. Once it's there, it's there in ink, for good. And if you and the other Girl Bosses you're doing business with put your signatures on the bottom, consider your business sealed and binding.

So what does that mean? It means working up certain formal invoices and agreements when you begin doing business with someone new. Discuss any terms you want to include—when you'll deliver products, how much you'll get paid (and when!)—beforehand. Use all your negotiating skills to work out the terms. Just listen, toss out your ideas, and keep bargaining until you come up with terms that work for you. Take notes when you're talking so you can keep track of your final decisions.

Then, later when you're chillin' on the couch, take your notes and organize them into some kind of logical form and print it out for both of you to sign. Once that's done, you'll have something to refer to if you ever forget whether you're supposed to ship new boxes of jeweled barrettes on the 1st or the 15th of the month. Plus you'll have a permanent record of your agreement if a shop you're dealing with says they only promised to pay you 15% when you know you agreed to 25%.

Don't get carried away with the kind of intense language you sometimes see in legal papers. Your contracts and invoices don't have to include words like **heretofore**, **insomuchas** or any reference to the **party of the second part.** Just get something down in plain English that's clear and accurate and you'll have the security of a written, signed document. Grab a folder and start a file to store all your paperwork.

Don't think you have to put anything in writing if you're dealing with friends and family? Think again. It's probably **most** important to sign a contract with your pals, because you'd never want a misunderstanding to hurt your relationship. Getting everything on paper will force you and your friend to think through every situation that could pop up. What happens, for instance, if you both set up a business and one of you wants out? Or suppose you want to bring in a third partner—how would the new ownership work? You would never want an unexpected development to break up your friendship, so be **real** Girl Bosses and sign on the dotted line.

Things to Include When You Put it in Writing

Who:	You and the people you're dealing with
What:	The work you're agreeing to do
When:	Dates that payments are due, dates you need to show up, deliver something, or finish a piece of work
How much:	What you'll get paid for a specific quantity of work
Details:	Any descriptions of the work you'll be doing that make it clear what you will and won't do—for example, if you're supposed to make a dozen beaded bracelets, describe the beads so later on there's no disagreement about whether they were supposed to be plastic or sterling silver
Signatures:	Yours and theirs

Stop Procrastinating!

Why Today Is Always Better

Solving Your Procrastinating Problems

Everyone is occasionally bitten by the lazy bug. It's understandable—you've got loads to do between school and friends and family. But you still want your business to be a success, so you've got to find ways to stay productive even when you're feeling unmotivated. If you trick yourself into pretending to work—when in reality you're getting zip accomplished—you're the one who will be disappointed in the end. So fight those urges when they pop up, or learn when to recognize the times when you just **can't** fight it. Here's how:

Work During Your Peak Hours

You probably already know whether you're a morning person or a night person. If you're lucky, maybe you're even both. At the very least, there is **some** time of day when you feel like you're at your peak. Some Girl Bosses can only get their mental juices flowing in the evening, when homework and all other distractions are behind. Some need to set aside a whole day—like a Saturday—to really focus on getting their businesses off the ground. Other diva bosses can fit in a few hours of work whenever—between classes, after school, on a weekend before going out with friends. None is better or worse than the other—the trick is to find the work pattern than suits you best. Work during your optimal times and you'll get the most done.

Know When It's Just Not Happening

Then again, there are times when you can't get anything done to save your life. You sit, you think, you rearrange the materials in the toolbox, or play a couple of computer games to get your fingers warmed up . . . and still nothing comes of it.

These are the times to cut yourself some slack, realize it's not going to happen, and leave your office and its contents behind. Sometimes it's a bigger waste of time to sit and get nothing done for hours than to leave the house and take a walk, work out, or wander through a bookstore. The worst thing you can do in this case is force it—you want to enjoy building your business, so if it gets to the point where it's no longer fun, take a day off from time to time. Come back to it when you're re-inspired.

Change Your Venue

Sometimes all it takes to get your motivation rolling is a change of scenery. Moving from your room to a coffee house down the block can be the difference between sitting staring at the ceiling and actually getting something done. If you feel like you've hit a wall of productivity in your main workspace, consider moving to a new location, temporarily. Of course, not all businesses can be moved that easily. But if you're designing fliers, going over your costs and profits, making lists of goals or supplies you need to purchase, or even putting together small crafts that can be transported easily, you can take them on the road.

You'll be amazed at how a change of scenery can revitalize your energy. Fight the rut. Look for ways to keep your work interesting and break the boundaries—that includes busting free from your office walls.

Than Tomorrow

Tips for Professional Procrastinators

✦ GATHER YOUR COMFORT SUPPLIES.
Get yourself a glass of water or soda and a snack before you start working and take them to your desk or workspace. That way you won't have an excuse to go tromping off to the kitchen when you get thirsty.

✦ CUT OUT DISTRACTIONS.
When you're in serious work mode, unplug the phone, turn on the answering machine, or ask your family to take messages for you—whatever you need for some uninterrupted time.

✦ SET UP A REWARD SYSTEM.
Set mini-goals, like writing a full page of text or making three pairs of earrings before you take a break. Then you can go for that phone call or a snack. That way your goal is finite and you'll have a reward waiting when you finish.

✦ DEFINE YOUR WORK BOUNDARY.
Work in an area of your room or in a part of the house that is designated as your official workspace. Don't use it for anything else. That way when you're in there, you'll mean business, and when you're **not** there, you won't even think about work.

✦ GIVE YOURSELF A TIME LIMIT.
Only work for that amount of time. If you tell yourself you're only working for another hour, it may help you concentrate **now.**

✦ ENLIST THE HELP OF A FRIEND.
This could really help on those days you're feeling especially unmotivated—it will make it more fun, and who knows, you may end up with a great business partner. (Just make sure you do more working than playing when you're together.)

Don't Worry So Much About Being Liked

This one is basic. Everyone wants to be liked, sure, but the hard truth is that we can't be liked by **everyone** all the time. Sometimes, the right decision for your business isn't the one that will make you most popular. That's what truly defines a Girl Boss: someone who's willing to take the heat for the sake of her business.

Suppose you've hired someone who's just not working out—not showing up, or not doing the work you've expected. Chances are you'll have to let her go. Why is that such a tough decision? That's easy—because you're afraid she won't like you if you fire her.

As a Girl Boss you'll find countless awkward spots like that one—sales people who want you to buy their product, even if it's not a good fit for your business. Or employees you can't pay as much as they'd like because of your tight budget. Or vendors you have to negotiate with for a lower price. Those are all situations where you'll have to put business before your personal relationships.

Real Girl Bosses learn to avoid taking business too personally. Think about what actors go through once they become successful—they see nasty gossip in (practically) every magazine they pick up. But they chalk that up to sour grapes or jealousy and move on. So should you! Focus on doing good work and everything else will fall into place.

Of course, that doesn't mean you should walk around being a first-class witch all the time. There's no reason you can't be pleasant while you're running your business, or even overly generous from time to time. It will help you build a good rapport with people when they think you're a no-pretenses, nice person. But every Girl Boss knows where to draw the line between being nice and being a chump. You'll learn the same thing yourself.

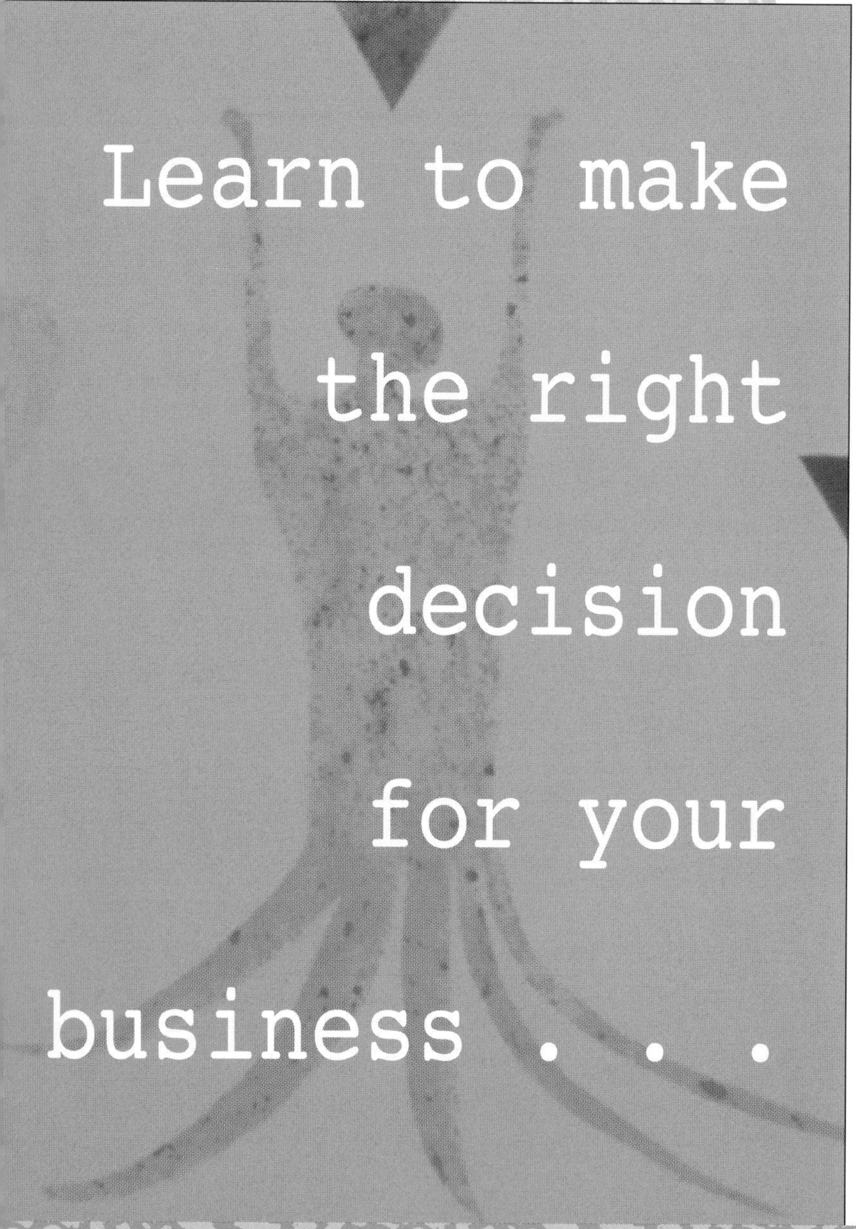

Learn to make the right decision for your business . . .

Well-behaved women

...Or About Being Scared

If you feel your stomach turning over on itself as you read this because you don't know how you can possibly be the cool boss you want to be, take heart. Everyone feels overwhelmed, scared, and confused—even the most powerful lady bosses in town.

First of all, remember there's a difference between being a little nervous and outright scared. Most of the time the little twinge you feel in your gut is a flutter of nervousness, and it will pass. As soon as you open your mouth and start speaking, that feeling will go away. If you're going to begin a performance or propose a business deal, you'll probably feel a little wave of anticipation. Breathe. Breathe again. Then jump in and before you know it you'll be negotiating like a wonder boss or singing your heart out. That nervousness will be a faint memory.

On the other hand, if you really are scared, try to figure out why. If it's just a small step on your road to success, consider ways to eliminate that part—but only temporarily. In other words, if it truly terrifies you to go back to a store to see how many of your beaded necklaces have sold, find someone else to do it for you the first couple of times. Then once you see how well they're selling and you're confidence is back, jump in and do it yourself.

The point is that being truly brave doesn't mean being fearless. Everyone has fears—they just learn to face them, conquer them, and move on. Don't let the scary stuff slow you down.

. . . not the one that will make you liked the most.

rarely make history.

—*Laurel Thatcher Ulrich*

Tanesha Egans

Tanesha Egans discovered cheerleading at Culver City High School and loved the chance it gave her to perform in front of crowds and learn to discipline herself. She had to keep her grades up and stay out of trouble, but her reward was that she loved what she was doing.

That started her thinking about how to spread the cheer. She began looking for an opportunity to coach younger teens during her junior year of high school and found almost 100 girls who were thrilled to have her as a coach. She began coaching cheerleading at an inner city school, hoping to give the kids there something to feel good about.

Soon she was running the whole show, helping teen girls through tryouts and instructing them on their routines. She even hung up her own cheerleading shoes to concentrate on coaching full-time. "It was a chance to be able to run things myself and show what I'd learned," Tanesha says, now 18. "It made me a leader."

Christy Haubegger,

like many great Girl Bosses, started her business to fill a gap in the marketplace. In 1996, at the age of 27, she founded the first bilingual magazine, *Latina*, because she saw a need for a unique publication and a strong voice for Hispanic women in the U.S. When Christy was growing up, she read women's magazines and felt like there was something missing: strong images and information that related to her experience as a Mexican-American teenager. She got her feet wet in publishing during law school when she joined the editorial staff of the *Stanford Law Review* and became its editor.

When she finished school, Christy set out to create a magazine that never existed before: a bilingual publication for women like her who juggle two cultures and two languages. She wrote a business plan and kept knocking on doors until she had a partner, Essence Communications Inc. Now Christy oversees all production and publishing aspects of *Latina*, which sells 300,000 copies of each issue.

Isabel Walcott

President and founder of SmartGirl Internette Inc.

Isabel was a Girl Boss back in seventh grade when she was making earrings with satin bows and selling them to her friends for $7 apiece. She kept that entrepreneurial spirit alive through high school, always thinking big. She looked around at available part-time jobs, but decided she wanted to start a business that would **really** bring in the bucks. She started cleaning houses for $12 to $14 an hour, and began thinking about how to expand. She went to a tennis club near her house in Milwaukee and passed out fliers and business cards to get clients. The best part was that she could set up a flexible work schedule: "I learned the freedom that could come from being your own boss," she says.

After college, Isabel joined her friend Wendy Kopp (see profile on page 30), working for **Teach for America** in its start-up phase. She watched and learned as the business grew, managing the accounting department. Most importantly, she knew when it was time to move on. She next worked for a a multi-media design and production company, learning every step of the way.

So a couple of years ago, when Isabel was ready to start **SMARTGIRL.COM**, she had all the tools she needed to make it a success. She spent a year working on the Web site by herself, keeping her expenses low and positioning herself to grow. The day she hired her first employee was "a great day because finally someone was helping me," she says. Check out smartgirl.com on the Web—your big ideas can come to fruition too.

Cosmetics Queen

L-to-R: Helena Rubenstein, Mary Brian, Sharon Lynn, and Mala Rubenstein, in 1934. Photo: Corbis/Bettman-UPI

Helena opened her first beauty salon in New York in 1914, trading on the success she'd already found in Europe. She built an empire on her cosmetics line by pioneering new trends for American women. She even helped to shape the images of movie stars during her day, and eventually became a true celebrity herself.

Helena Rubenstein

Being a Good Negotiator

LEARNING THE ART OF NEGOTIATION is not as hard as it sounds. It's really a matter of knowing when to hold your ground, when to give in, and when to ask for more. Negotiating is the art of mastering subtleties and remembering that sometimes it's better to give up a little something in order to get something even better.

ONE AREA where you'll find yourself negotiating a lot: **price.** Customers will try to negotiate with you for a lower price, or you may find yourself negotiating for a better deal from a supply store. You'll also find yourself negotiating in other ways—like with stores to get your goods displayed.

AN EASY WAY to come to negotiated decisions is to think big—as in, look for opportunities to buy and sell in bulk. Bulk orders will give you leverage to set a better price from a supplier. The same goes for customers who agree to place big orders from **you.** In exchange for guaranteed business, most good Girl Bosses will offer a discount.

The Negotiating Basics

- ☛ Stick to your guns
- ☛ Ask for what you want
- ☛ Know your limits
- ☛ Work out a compromise that makes both parties happy

How to Get What You Want

Girl Bosses Can Negotiate!

Because of their age-long training in human relations—for that is what feminine intuition really is—women have a special contribution to make to any group enterprise, and I feel it is up to them to contribute the kinds of awareness that relatively few men . . . have incorporated through their education.

—MARGARET MEAD,
Blackberry Winter

QUIZ—Are You a Good Negotiator?

1 *You walk into a store and ask if they want to display your pottery dishes on consignment. They tell you they'll do it if they can keep 75% of the purchase price, more than any other store. You:*

A Tell them the going rate is 50%—take it or leave it.

B Offer to let them keep 75% on the first 10 dishes that sell and drop to 45% on everything after that.

C Figure keeping 25% yourself is better than nothing and agree to their terms.

2 *You're buying supplies at a craft store to make your first batch of jeweled barrettes. You:*

A Ask to talk to the manager and explain that you plan to buy all your supplies at this store, so you'd like to work out a deal for a bulk discount.

B Ask whether they give discounts for large purchases or steady customers—if they don't, you'll pay full price.

C Ask for a discount and leave if you don't get one, figuring you'll always be able to find a store that offers you a better deal.

3 *You're selling your jeweled barrettes in stores and business is going quite well. Some friends at school ask if they can buy them directly from you or even have a few for free. You:*

A Tell them which stores they can find them in and ask them to buy them there.

B Offer them a discount for buying directly from you and offer an even bigger discount if they buy five at a time.

C Worry that they'll ditch your friendship if you don't give them some free samples.

Answers

1 **B.** Your initial instinct may be to tell the store to take 50% or forget the whole thing, but you might be able to get a better deal if you wheel and deal a little bit. Tell the store manager that the going rate is 50% but that you'll make an exception until you've proven yourself. Offer to let the store keep 75% of the purchase price on the first few items they sell, just so they'll have faith that your goods have selling power. But then, once you've proven yourself, tell them you'd like them to accept the going rate or even a little less—like 45% to compensate for the initial steep cut in profits you've taken.

2 **A.** Stores will often give you a discount on supplies for buying in bulk or for establishing yourself as a steady customer. Find out if the store has this kind of arrangement. If not, ask if they'll set one up with you. Never make threats about taking your business elsewhere unless you know for a fact you can get a better deal someplace else. (If you could, you'd take it, right?) Just negotiate like a pro—some stores will take you even more seriously when you approach them with the desire to negotiate.

3 **B.** Remind your friends that you're taking your business seriously so freebies are out of the question. But do offer them a healthy discount for buying the barrettes directly from you. Remember that you'd be giving 50% of your revenues to a store that carries your barrettes, so you can offer your friends up to 50% off and walk away with the same profit. Encourage them to be your best customers because the more people who are out there wearing your barrettes, the better chance you'll have of starting a major trend.

Keeping Your Perspective—

Once you've got your business rolling, it seems like you should just be able to let it run. But the trick is striking that delicate balance between running your business and letting your business run **you.**

Sure, you want to succeed, but not at the cost of your sanity, your friendships, your grades, or your health. Remember to keep an eye on all these other pieces of your life, so when your business soars into the stratosphere, you'll REALLY have it all.

Most of all, you've got to remember to be kind to yourself. That may sound obvious, but you'd be surprised how easy it is to beat yourself up when you don't meet your goals instantly. Don't do it. Keep an eye on your goal, but live in the real world. You're already going above and beyond what most people set out to do at your age, so if it doesn't come together instantly, cut yourself some slack.

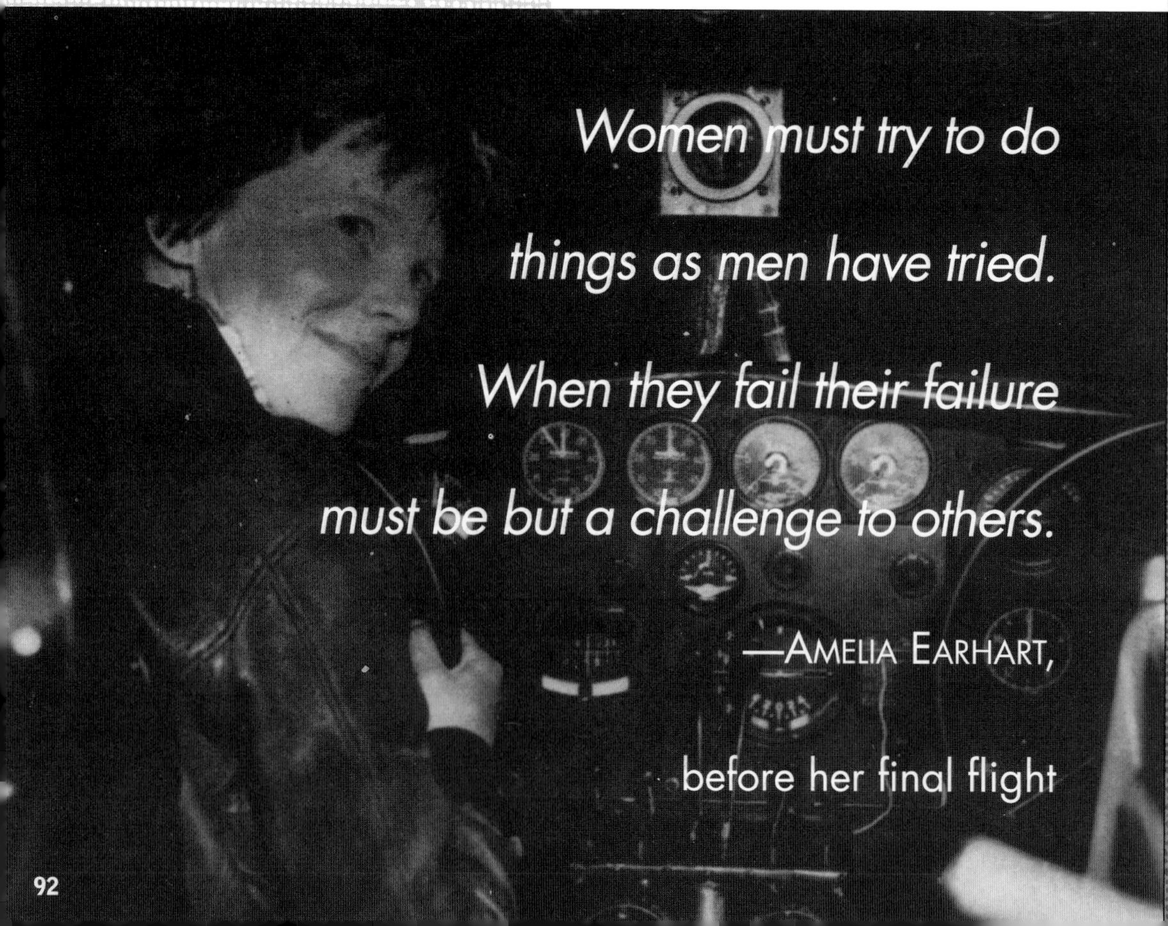
Women must try to do
things as men have tried.
When they fail their failure
must be but a challenge to others.
—Amelia Earhart,
before her final flight

QUIZ: Are Yo

1 On your first day to take samples of your home grown cilantro, rosemary and sage to sell at a local farmers market, you learn that you need a permit to sell there. You:

- **A** Hear a voice in your head saying you should have known better, that a REAL Girl Boss would have known everything before she set out.
- **B** Get so frustrated with yourself that you throw your herbs in the trash and storm home.
- **C** Figure out where to get a sellers permit.

2 You've gotten your permit and spent an entire day selling your herbs. You've sold all of them and have worked up quite a sweat—and an appetite. You:

- **A** Take a small portion of your profits and take yourself to an affordable lunch.
- **B** Tell yourself you shouldn't stop for food because you need to get back to the garden supply store and buy more seeds to plant.
- **C** Tell yourself you won't deserve a splurge on a restaurant lunch until you've met a lofty sales target.

ANSWERS:

1 Pick C! The defeatist attitude shown in answers A and B is no way to be a good boss or a good supporter of your own endeavor. Pick answer C and move forward, rather than getting stopped in your tracks by negative thinking.

2 A is the best answer. You've worked hard and met your sales target for the day—you've sold everything. Get some lunch. Look over yours sales totals and celebrate a successful sales day. Answers B and C will only force you to reach higher and higher targets before you'll admit you deserve a break and some celebration. Do not get sucked into that kind of thinking. Celebrate small victories!

So There.

Just because you set out to be a great diva boss, doesn't mean you'll do it perfectly right off the bat. And you'd be surprised to hear who may get the worst treatment in your early days as a Girl Boss: **you.** That's because you may overwork yourself, or push yourself to do things before you're ready. Don't put yourself down if you don't come out like some goddess boss right from the start.

You're your own biggest booster and all the positive feedback you want for your business should come first from you. Here are some tips to make sure you're treating your most important employee—you—the right way:

Keep a record of your goals, and divide each one into mini-goals.

Check off your progress. Make a check mark by each mini-goal as you achieve it so you have a visible record of your progress.

Reward yourself. Each time you reach a certain number of accomplished goals—you decide how many you want it to be—give yourself a reward. It could be splurging on something small that you wouldn't ordinarily buy, or taking a break to spend a couple hours with your best gal-pal.

Don't give yourself negative reinforcement. It's so easy to beat yourself up and call yourself a failure for not being an instant success. But why is this the case? Learn to recognize your "inner critic" and stop it whenever it rears its annoying head.

Make sure you have a life. No matter how much you want to succeed—and this goes for school and any other goals you set for yourself—keep a balance in your life. (But don't take too much goofing-around time either! The point is never to do too much of any one thing, even something that seems really great.)

You get the idea—BE GOOD TO YOURSELF! Try to give yourself silent encouragement for all your hard work, no matter how long it takes to succeed.

(More) Advice from Girl Bosses:

Learn How to Get Out of a Bind Gracefully

If you ever find yourself in a situation where things are going nowhere—or worse—downhill fast, there are a few things you can do to extract yourself so you'll have time to think, call someone for help, or come up with a plan.

- Say you need to run for now, but ask if you can resume the discussion later over the phone.
- If you're on the phone and the conversation is escalating into an argument, say you've just gotten called into a meeting and ask if you can call back in a couple of minutes.
- If you have a disagreement over price, say you'll go back and look at your paperwork and get back to the person soon.
- Smile, remain calm and say, "I'm sure we can work something out."

Girl Boss Rule

Stamp Out Your Inner Critic

She's there, lurking, ready to jump out if you make a mistake or take on more responsibility than you can handle. But she's essentially harmless. She's no match for you. You, after all, are the boss, and any criticism she can dish out you can handle, no problem.

Everyone has that little voice that says you should have known, or that you should have said something differently—that you should have been *better somehow.* And, even worse, that little voice is worst when you're most insecure—it really knows which buttons to push. But when you hear that annoying whine ("You're not talented enough for that job"), cut it short. Listen long enough to recognize it for what it is—your insecurities voicing themselves—and then remind yourself that everything will be fine.

The most important way to shut up your inner critic is with a dose of positive reinforcement. Remind yourself of your many successes, and applaud yourself for what a great job you've done. That inner critic is no match for you.

Laura Groppe started her company, Girl Games, in 1994 because there were no great CD-ROM games for girls. Laura used her entertainment background—she spent seven years co-producing and directing short films and features—to give her CD-ROMs and Web sites a professional look. She saw an opening where nothing existed and figured out a way to fill it with great interactive products like "Let's Talk About Me" and "Teen Digital Diva" CD-ROMs. Check out her Web site at www.shredbetty.net and www.planetgirl.com.

Take Debate!

Ever wonder how those really powerful lady bosses seem so cool under pressure, or why they're so good at delivering a speech? Chances are, they took debate. Don't miss your chance to become just as savvy in front of a crowd. If your school offers debate classes, sign up!

Debate is more than a slightly dweeby credit on your school transcript. It's the chance to learn to communicate your ideas in a convincing, forceful way. Now *that's* what a Girl Boss needs to know. And it's not only for public speakers—debate teaches you to take a position, and gather information to back it up. That means you'll be more persuasive in small meetings, and even one-on-one. Debate also teaches you great organizational skills because you're required to take all the information you've compiled and to put it into some kind of order that makes sense.

You'll get a chance to think on your feet, as your opponent challenges your positions and asks you to back them up with facts. The best part is that you'll get over any fears of speaking. Every Girl Boss knows how to make her point, whether it's to one person or a thousand.

Other Books from GIRL PRESS

COOL WOMEN

The Thinking Girl's Guide to the Hippest Women in History

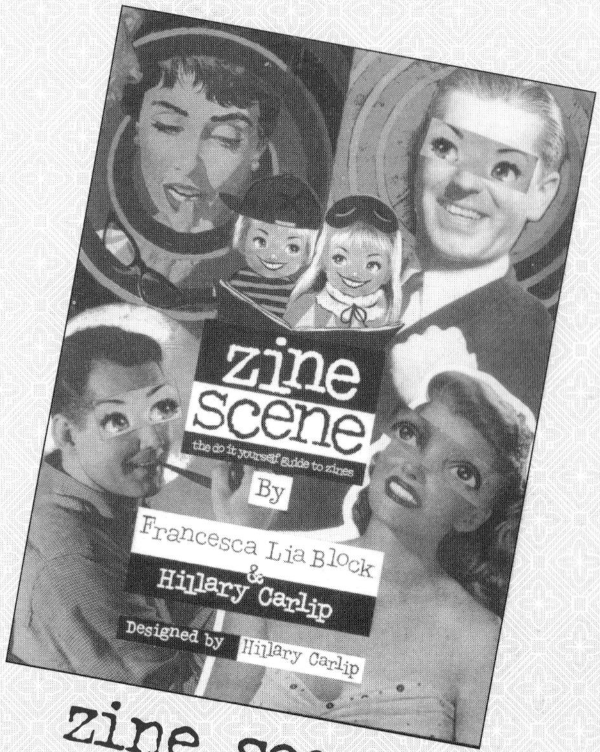

zine scene

The Do It Yourself Guide to Zines

Coming SOON!

The Real Rules for Girls

Notes from the Hippest Aunt You Never Had

One Model's Life

(It's Not Easy Being Thin)

A Send-up of the Supermodel World

I'm not afraid of storms for I'm learning how to sail my ship.

—Louisa May Alcott

Always the pushiest one on the playground

The publisher, Pam

Still does this when her writing gets edited

The writer, Stacy

The designer, Amy

Always had the best crayon sets